Collecting Traditional American Basketry

E. P. DUTTON | NEW YORK

Collecting Traditional American Basketry

GLORIA ROTH TELEKI

---

*To artisans and others
who love folk crafts*

CONTENTS

Color plates follow page 70.

LIST OF COLOR PLATES AND FIGURES

NOTE: Dimensions given in the captions include measurements taken at about the widest point. These can vary considerably over the surface of a basket—for example, in diameter—because of irregularities intrinsic in handwork, uneven drying of the materials after completion, placement of attachments such as handles, and warping or other damage that has resulted from use or the passage of time. O.H. means overall height and includes handles. H. is the height of a basket that has no handle and includes any cover.

Baskets not credited are from private collections.

Color Plate

1. *Clam basket*
2. *Fisherman's creel/trout basket*
3. *Open-sided oval basket*

Figure

PREFACE

Collecting Traditional American Basketry is, in effect, a supplement to my earlier book, *The Baskets of Rural America,* which was published by E.P. Dutton in 1975. After I'd wrapped up that effort, I kept on researching and buying, always having in mind the possibility of a follow-up work to hold what was left over and what I'd find later. The present volume has been written to cover just that, as well as to respond to the needs and interests expressed by the readers of its gratifyingly well-received predecessor.

I have been able to illustrate here some basket types only described in my previous writing, among them pack/backpack and cotton baskets. Included are information and examples from Hawaii and Alaska and the Caribbean island Commonwealth of Puerto Rico. A tour around Lake Michigan yielded most of the Western Great Lakes Indian baskets taken up in the "Native Peoples" chapter. Other travels provided samplings from numerous additional tribal groups: Southwest to Southeast and into New York State, and present-day black white-oak splint weavers in the Deep South, as well as Afro-American coiled pieces garnered during another trip into Charleston County, South Carolina, a favorite collecting ground.

A good deal more journeying has been done for me by dealers who brought back or put me onto choice old examples when they encountered them; several such may be seen in these pages. I have quite a few active basketmakers to thank for excellent new ones, some made to order, and for filling my commissions for copies of particular kinds.

I have been asked about coiled-straw *skeps*, or beehives, and basketry other than containers, so some of these are presented, too. Unusual utilitarian baskets I'd noticed during museum visits but had been unable to include before appear now, as does a small selection of wonderful and extremely valuable pieces: Datsolalee's Washo masterpiece (fig. 21), a Pomo feather-covered coiled basket in brilliant color (pl. 5), and fine Attu (Aleut) twined-grass containers (fig. 78).

When I began to receive lecture invitations, the nature and sources of the inquiries confirmed that three segments existed among my readership: first, as expected, the antiques collectors, curators, and dealers; next, the practicing craftspeople themselves and those who simply appreciated handmade things; and finally, the folklife and culture researchers, whose response was surprisingly strong.

Serious folklife studies are a recent importation of a European discipline that "has penetrated American academia, both directly from Scandinavian sources and indirectly from the British Isles, where the term folklife is used for scholarly journals, societies, and university programs." [1] Although the term had seldom been heard in the United States until recent years, many individuals have had enough interest to delve into the subject less formally, and the personal nature of its material holds potential appeal for vast numbers of others who could be reached through expanded exhibits, film, and publications, as well as at restored or re-created villages, communities, homesteads, or the living historical farms that keep popping up in travel articles.

Collecting Traditional American Basketry has been planned to stand alone. It does not duplicate the text or examples shown in *The Baskets of Rural America,* but the discussion and full captions give essential background material. For the current book, we have maintained the high-quality photography and careful reproduction commented upon by the first volume's users, and, by popular suggestion, we are including sixteen pages of color plates.

In the few years since publication of *The Baskets of Rural America,* basketry has won a somewhat belated but spreading recognition as an American folk art. It has been attracting heightened attention from collectors and museums; as an antiques dealer informed me, all innocent of my identity: "I think baskets are coming to the front now!" The present volume has been designed to enlarge upon the topic of "Collecting Traditional American Basketry," to offer "more" to enthusiasts who are growing in interest and numbers.

ACKNOWLEDGMENTS

I should like to express my sincere appreciation to everyone who has contributed to this undertaking by providing information or photographs, lending baskets, or opening their private gardens and homes as settings for color photography. Among the last-mentioned are Mr. and Mrs. A. John Ortseifen of Lake Forest, Illinois, whose lovely stone wall appears on the front cover.

Of the many expert informants who responded to my inquiries for advice or specimens, Professor Eugenio Fernández-Méndez of the Department of Anthropology at the University of Puerto Rico in San Juan must be singled out for particular recognition, not only for his invaluable assistance but for his sustained enthusiasm and persistence through a lengthy correspondence.

I am especially indebted to my editor, Cyril I. Nelson, and to Nelson D. (Dave) Rodelius of E.P.S. Studios in Evanston, Illinois, for their personal absorption with this project. Their collaboration on *The Baskets of Rural America* was a most fortunate circumstance that has been duplicated with their participation in this volume. Mr. Nelson's presence gives assurance of achieving a better book. Mr. Rodelius, who did the great bulk of the black-and-white illustrations and all the color photography except plate 5 and the back cover, is a photographer whose excellent work is matched by his suggestions; it is a pleasure to work with such fine material.

The captions give some specific credits to other photographers, institutions, and collectors. Several of the active basketmakers whose pieces are shown here were as generous in sharing background and practical knowledge as they were in willingness to make up baskets for me, and I do thank them for both.

For the following additional listings, many representing associations of long standing, I can name only those individuals who helped most with the current volume and shall do so alphabetically: Barbara Beckos, formerly Curator of Education, Everson Museum of Art, Syracuse, New York; Joanne Segal Brandford, Research Fellow in the Textile Arts, Peabody Museum of Archaeology and Ethnology, Cambridge, Massachusetts; Ted J. Brasser, Canadian Ethnology Service, National Museum of Man, National Museums of Canada, Ottawa, Ontario, Canada; Walter R. Brown, Madaket, Nantucket, Massachusetts; Jerold L. Collings, Director, Gila River Arts and Crafts Center, Sacaton, Arizona; Cindy Davies, Assistant Curator, Heard Museum, Phoenix, Arizona; Greg Day, Sullivan's Island, South Carolina; Genny R. de Rivera, Occupational Therapy Consultant, Junta de Servicios Communales a Ciudadanos de Mayor Edad, Inc., Puerto Nuevo and Santurce, Puerto Rico; Betty DuPree, Qualla Arts & Crafts Mutual, Inc., Cherokee, North Carolina; Susan W. Fair, General Manager, The Alaska Native Arts & Crafts Cooperative Association, Inc., Anchorage, Alaska; Virginia Frank, Manager, Miccosukee Arts and Crafts Center, Tamiami Trail west of Miami, Florida; Woodson Gannaway, Mountain View, Arkansas; Henry J. Harlow, Chief Curator, Old Sturbridge Village, Sturbridge, Massachusetts; Carroll J. Hopf, Director, Pennsylvania Farm Museum of Landis Valley,

Lancaster, Pennsylvania; Lucia H. Jaycocks, Mount Pleasant, South Carolina; Br. Theodore E. Johnson, The United Society of Shakers, Sabbathday Lake, Poland Spring, Maine; Joyce A. Korbecki, Scientific Assistant, Department of Anthropology, Field Museum of Natural History, Chicago, Illinois; Harriett G. Lawrence, Country Store Manager, Georgia Agrirama, Tifton, Georgia; Karen L. MacCullen, The Alaska Native Arts & Crafts Cooperative Association, Inc., Anchorage, Alaska; Shirley McGill, Geneva, Illinois; Isabel M. McIntosh, Assistant Registrar, Indian Department, Philbrook Art Center, Tulsa, Oklahoma; Jeanne McKown, Information Officer, Georgia Bureau of Industry and Trade, Atlanta, Georgia; Claude Medford, Jr., formerly Manager, Coushatta Cultural Center, Elton, Louisiana; Sue Meddock, Assistant to the President, The Balloon Works, Statesville, North Carolina; John Harlow Ott, Director, Hancock Shaker Village, Pittsfield, Massachusetts; E. D. Pawling, Greenwillow Farm, Chatham, New York; Maggie Poncho and her family, Livingston, Texas; Florence Pohley Ritz, Mauldin, South Carolina; Madeline Roemig, Director, Museum of Amana History, Amana, Iowa; Joanna E. Schanz, West Amana, Iowa; Seth M. Schindler, Assistant Curator, Arizona State Museum, University of Arizona, Tucson, Arizona; Catherine Solomon, Choctaw Craft Association, Philadelphia, Mississippi; Ben Stone, Curator of American Indian Art, Philbrook Art Center, Tulsa, Oklahoma; Jane and Phillip Tarbell, Delmar, New York; Beatrice K. Taylor, Librarian, and her Assistant, Christine Edmonson, The Joseph Downs Manuscript and Microfilm Collection, The Henry Francis du Pont Winterthur Museum, Winterthur, Delaware; Dr. James W. VanStone, Curator of North American Archaeology and Ethnology, Department of Anthropology, Field Museum of Natural History, Chicago, Illinois; and David H. Wood, Nantucket and Stockbridge, Massachusetts.

Most of all, I am grateful to my husband Deneb for his involvement and unfailing encouragement and to our son David, who faithfully carried out supportive tasks.

Collecting Traditional American Basketry

INTRODUCTION

Anonymity has long been the usual lot of the basketmaker. In the beginning, which is believed to predate the development of pottery, production was meant simply for the creator's own use. Later, professional artisans came to be known only in their immediate areas and seldom identified their work.

We'll never find the first baskets made on this continent. It seems safe to assume that they were temporary, sacklike contrivances that were devised as spontaneously as the need had arisen to transport some found food—berries, mussels, roots, eggs, birds or small animals killed—and as readily discarded, disintegrating and turning quickly to dust. But basketry artifacts recovered from the protective environments of southwestern caves have been radiocarbon-dated to nine thousand years,[2] a greater age than those from archaeological digs anywhere else on earth. Although we cannot with certainty identify their

1

makers' descendants, they are probably still making baskets today, as are members of some fifty American Indian tribes.

The oldest fragments discovered had been made by *twining,* a method in which two or more flexible horizontal elements are twisted together between the warps or verticals; depending upon their materials, twined baskets can be very fine and soft (Aleut grasswork) or crude and extremely strong (burden baskets and desert water bottles). At a more recent archaeological level, *coiling* was retrieved, a technique involving a core foundation of strands or rods stitched with a binding into a spiral. A third method is *plaiting:* thin, flat strips interwoven at right angles. (When the warp, or vertical element, is more rigid than the weft, or horizontal element, the construction may be referred to as *wickerwork.*) A detailed discussion of weaving techniques, accompanied by drawings providing visual reference, appears in Charles E. Rozaire's "A Curator's Note," published in *Indian Basketry of Western North America* (1977), which is an exhibition catalogue for the Charles W. Bowers Memorial Museum, Santa Ana, California.

The first Americans had to carry everything on their own backs. Basketry was natural: just about anything botanical that grew could be transformed into a basket; it was practical: sturdy and light in weight; and it could be adapted and turned into tools, clothing and ornament, shelter, and even weaponry.

Contact with whites caused basketmaking to change to please these new customers, especially to support oneself when the foreign presence had disrupted and then destroyed the old ways of subsistence for the Indians left behind when the frontier pushed ever westward. The newcomers had become settlers; they had put down roots and, having established themselves, set their culture up as the mainstream one.

Inevitably, intermarriage led to exchanges of basketry techniques and design modifications. The pursuit of basketmaking by whole families was especially efficient, as youths and the elderly could participate in the lengthy and tiring procurement of materials or the monotonous preparation of quantities of vegetal stuff, several kinds of which may be needed for the various constituent parts of one basket. Usable plants are legion, most gathered from the wild, cleaned, and woven fresh, whereas others involve cultivation, curing, and/or storage for later use.

Interesting effects can be achieved solely with the natural colors of the fibers; although indigenous basketmakers have also brewed dyes and applied decorations, non-Indians have seldom done so.

Most artisans concentrate on one method and, usually, one sort of material—*splint:* flat ribbons of wood or other heavy fiber; *rods:* willow and other twigs; or *grasses:* used in twining or as a bundle to form the core foundation for coiling. The essential tools for basketry can be few, one's hands and a knife or other sharp implement. A lone craftsman may complete one basket at a time or take a number of them together through each procedure, but when a group of people share production, they generally practice specialization in tasks. The work is, in practice, somewhat seasonal, partly because plant growth is, and, although the actual weaving could theoretically be done almost any time (unless humidity is a vital factor), it requires some freedom from agricultural chores that is usually enjoyed in a rural setting only during the winter months.

Communities of basketmakers were once common. Today, the Afro-Americans of Charleston County, South Carolina, and the Lightship Basket weavers of Nantucket Island, Massachusetts, continue to produce. The only remaining communities of basketmakers to be found in the lower forty-eight states exist on Indian reservations or in concentrations such as one very small town in northern Michigan (Peshabestown) that is made up of households of mixed Chippewa and Ottawa lineage.

However, scattered basketweavers persevere in the Northeast and the South. Most were taught by parents or other relatives and have been making baskets since their childhoods, sturdy pack baskets, plain baskets for gathering eggs or picking cotton, for going to market or carrying pies to socials.

FIGURE 1. The ultimate utility basket: gentlemen ballooning, suspended in a large wicker basket, also variously called a gondola, car, cradle, or carriage. Although this photograph is French and dated July 18, 1865, ballooning has been enjoying a "buoyant renaissance," as *Time* magazine recently put it in an article on hot-air sport ballooning in America. Photograph courtesy America Hurrah Antiques, New York City.

FUNCTIONALITY
AND FORM

The kind of farm and country life that called for baskets aplenty to gather and store the fruits of the land must seem to many rather like a shadowy memory of grandparents past. It should come as no surprise that by far the great preponderance of the current output of "working" baskets is going to be sold to collectors. Some are, indeed, kept in the homes of the basketmakers, say, to fetch a few potatoes for dinner or, yes, to pick that cotton on small family-owned patches that still exist in the Deep South, or for washing boiled hominy in an Iroquois kitchen. But the only commercial application of hand-woven baskets that I've come across recently was at a pick-your-own apple orchard in Maine, where the management had set out handled, wide-splint round baskets for customers to fill for fun; the clerk said a local man had made them.

To a traditional basketmaker, functionality is the chief justification for a basket's existence, with the job determining its shape and how great its capacity need be, and the plants at hand and the maker's ingenuity are the other determinants. Some forms have been planned to handle a particular chore, while many service baskets have been put to multiple ends. One may find new baskets even more skillfully fashioned than a lot of the old yeoman kind, yet no more useful or better able to survive hard, regular use. Carefully finished splints aren't essential to a stalwart basket intended for bringing in the dirty root vegetables or taking out the clean wash.

Illustrated in this chapter is an array of generally plain-and-honest special-purpose utility baskets, although the fact that he or she was making a riddle didn't deter one basketmaker from managing to turn out a practical object while pleasuring the eye, too.

Admittedly, balloon baskets—the kind you go aloft in (figs. 1, 2)— are hardly an everyday part of today's life-style, but it seems that there are now a thousand hot-air balloons in the United States and some

FIGURE 2. Workshop for basketry carriages at hot-air sport-balloon factory in North Carolina: 1974. The text discussion provides information. Photograph courtesy The Balloon Works, Statesville, North Carolina.

three times as many adventurous hobbyists licensed by the Federal Aviation Administration to pilot them. Unaware that I happened to be in Albuquerque, New Mexico, while the 1977 International Hot-Air Balloon Fiesta was getting underway, I found myself swept with delight as the bluest sky suddenly filled with huge, colorfully patterned spheres. And hanging from them were baskets—of people!

Investigation revealed that American balloon manufacturers have their basketry carriages (in all honesty, some gondolas are aluminum) woven locally, either at their factory site or subcontracted nearby, in order to assure quality control and careful compliance with stringent Federal Aviation Administration regulations. They buy rattan, generally imported from the Philippines, although an English manufacturer employs willow because cultivated Dutch osiers are readily available there. Perhaps two hundred and fifty basketry balloon-cars are sold in the world annually. Although some are the customary rectangle, a leading designer laid out a unique sculpted triangular model for facility and comfortable allocation of the closely restricted space.

Why basketry? It is obvious that weight must be kept to a minimum, so basketry certainly fills that bill. Yet, because the aeronauts' safety is paramount, one designer (Tracy Barnes of The Balloon Works, Statesville, North Carolina, in a reprinting from *Ballooning*, the journal of the Balloon Federation of America) has addressed the critical question as follows:

> *The strength requirements for a balloon basket are relatively severe. Most modern airplanes, for example, have a certified payload that is only a fraction of the weight of the structure itself, and a plane that is certified to carry a payload equivalent to its own weight is considered exceptional. In contrast the FireFly7 is certified by the F. A. A. for a gross load of 1660 lbs.—11.8 times the weight of the 4.0T basket! Our model 4.0T, 4.5T and 5.0T have passed static load tests of over 3400 lbs. or over 23 times basket weight.*

Additional points are made: basketry, being a nonconductor, eliminates electrical hazard from power-line contact and can cushion the

FIGURE 3. Eel trap/eelpot and eel's-view close-up of entrance; complete with wooden stopper, iron weight or sinker tied onto side, and two-cork float: 75–100 years old. A cone-shaped insert is woven separately, with the bottom open and the splints almost touching at the tip but not fastened together; then it is bound to the larger rim of the open-ended cylinder, pointing inside. The wooden stopper is jammed tightly into the other end (on some, a bag is tied on, instead). The trap is laid on the ocean floor, anchored by the attached weight, with the float bobbing on the surface to mark its location. The eel, attracted by the rotting meat placed as bait in the chamber, swims through the funnel and isn't bright enough to push his way back through the splint tips that have fallen closed behind him. The fisherman, when checking his traps, hauls up the whole device and pulls out the stopper to take his catch. Basketry traps for fish and eels are still being made in the South, where fresh-water eels are caught in streams and lakes. H. without stopper 21"; Outside diam. (entrance end) 7"; Cone L. 15".

FIGURE 4. Fur trapper's pack basket, osiers (willow rods): mid-nineteenth century. Full-time professionals, as well as lots of part-timers who wanted to supplement their regular farming income with the lucrative sale of pelts, tramped winter trap lines with their provisions and gear stashed in baskets that were worn on their backs by means of straps through which the arms slipped. Splint backpack baskets have been commoner and continue to be made by both the Passamaquoddy of Maine and the Mohawks of upper New York State, as well as by individuals in the Adirondacks and their foothills (see fig. 65). This example has a widened opening; others are normally narrowed in. H. 18"; Opening 18½" x 15¾". Photograph courtesy the New York State Historical Association, Cooperstown, New York.

pilot and passengers from injury during landings or collisions with obstacles during flight. But the salient argument is that "The forces encountered during relatively high velocity impacts are best distributed throughout a structure by a framework that can flex, absorb and dampen the impact."

Moving along to more mundane occupations, we come to baskets for catching or carrying nature's marine bounty: the complete eel-trap rig of figure 3 (its caption has a full explanation), a clam-gathering basket with openwork wire bottom (pl. 1), and a fisherman's creel with hand-carved wooden lid that has been scratched with the legal trout length (pl. 2). Backpack baskets have borne a fur trapper's supplies and equipment (fig. 4) or become part of a sportsman's more elegant outfit; one popular for recreational use but fully suitable for professionals may be seen in figure 65. These have been fitted with cloth harnesses that pass over the shoulders and under the arms, but straps of leather or ropes have sufficed for others. A few individuals in the Northeast supply backpack baskets; others are offered by the Mohawks at the Akwesasne–St. Regis Reservation at the New York–Canadian border; and they are among the utility baskets of the Passamaquoddy tribe that are widely sold in Maine.

FIGURE 5. High-legged (four carefully carved 4″ bowlegs) basket, probably for rinsing wool; ash, with original rawhide lashing on rim: early to mid-nineteenth century. Freshly sheared wool was washed in a strong, hot solution, then thoroughly rinsed by setting a basketful in flowing water. Legs and an openwork bottom facilitated the flushing and air-drying afterward. The baskets more frequently had a pair of handles rather than slots, and splint bindings were normal. The handsomest example of its type that I've seen. H. 14″; Diam. 20″–21″ (slightly ovoid).

FIGURE 6. Rare six-legged basket, ash with openwork bottom, from the Northeast: fourth quarter of the nineteenth century. This was most likely meant as a laundry/wash/clothes basket; however, short-legged baskets sometimes stored root vegetables in the underground cellar as this kind of bottom permitted air circulation and cut down spoilage. The basket shows off pillows covered with sections salvaged from worn patchwork quilts; the Flower Basket pattern in variations with fruit or flowers (I have seen a pretty one with pastel eggs) is one of the most favored. A four-stamp commemorative block honoring "Folk Art USA: Quilts," with a basket pattern in different fabrics, was issued by our Postal Service in 1978. O.H. 13"; L. 28"; W. 19".

In those long-ago days when newly clipped wool was washed in a fast-running stream or under a waterfall, high-legged baskets did the job. Although it is rare to find one outside a museum, the specimen in figure 5 was a fortunate acquisition, doubly so because it is handsome, an attribute generally absent among its kind. The shorter-legged basket in figure 6 has a rare set of six legs and was probably a laundry basket, once a necessity for every household. Also unusual is a baby's partially covered bed basket (fig. 7).

FIGURE 7. Baby's partially covered bed basket, ash splint: nineteenth century. Visible lying inside is a separate plaited piece for covering the open end to keep drafts away from the infant. L. 39″; W. 22″. Photograph courtesy the New York State Historical Association, Cooperstown, New York.

FIGURE 9. Fruit-picking basket bound to heavy wooden dowel, into which three of the strong ribs have been inserted, and a rope would have been tied on as in the replacement: a good century old. The flattened back is slightly incurved. Curator Carroll J. Hopf (see Selected Bibliography) found a larger one in Ohio in the early 1960s, its possessor stating that a ninety-year-old man's grandparents had been the original owners and that it had been used primarily for harvesting apples. The picker would sling the rope over his shoulder and climb up into the tree with his basket aboard. H. 13″; Back to front 8″; Dowel L. 13″.

Some robust German went into the orchards of upstate New York with my bowed-back apple-picking basket (fig. 8) tied to his middle. See figure 9 for another singular fruit-picking basket, of rib-type construction and bound onto a thick wooden dowel to which a rope had been fastened so that it could be worn by the picker while up in the tree. Apples were the staple fruit just about everywhere; their slicing and drying were common autumn activities accomplished in several

FIGURE 8. Bowed-back apple-picking basket from upstate New York not far from the St. Lawrence Seaway, twilled bottom: third quarter of the nineteenth century. The piece is said to have belonged to German settlers in the area, where orchards yet flourish. O.H. 11¾″; L. 25″; Across rim from deepest incurve of back to front handle 14½″.

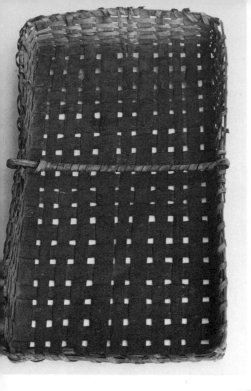

FIGURE 10. Sliced-apple drying basket, black ash; openwork bottom to increase exposure and hasten the process. The basket would have been placed on the windowsill, half inside and half out in the sun. Notice the flat handle crossing the basket; it was made of four strips of splint bound around with another splint. (Baskets for fish were similar but at least a foot deep.) L. 44″; W. 22″; D. 4½″. Photograph courtesy of the Mary Earle Gould Collection, Hancock Shaker Village, Hancock, Massachusetts.

FIGURE 11. Riddle, for separating out the large straws from the grain heads or spikes, coarse-openwork sieve bottom: early nineteenth century. Here is a real beauty! I've not previously encountered an octagonal base; six-sided bottoms, however, are normal with hexagonal-openwork weave. O.H. 9½″; Diam. 22″. Photograph courtesy Old Sturbridge Village, Sturbridge, Massachusetts.

ways, from festooning strings of cored slices about the ceiling beams to resting shallow basketfuls on the windowsill, half outside at a time (fig. 10).

A really fine *riddle*—a coarse sieve for dividing the broken-off heavy stalks from the grain spikes—that is perfectly tailored to the task and yet fulfills that old cliché, "a delight to the eye," rests at Old Sturbridge Village in Sturbridge, Massachusetts (fig. 11).

FIGURE 12. Three-handled basket that could be carried in several ways, black ash: copy of one in a museum made by Wayne Rundell of Brooklyn, Connecticut, in 1977. When heavily loaded, a person could lift it with a hand at each end handle, or two people could share the carrying, one at each end, while one could manage a light load with the center handle alone. A New England museum once commissioned six of these reproductions for inclusion in their store exhibit. The craftsman, who also works with white oak, here uses heavier splint and has made the weavers narrower, resulting in a stronger basket than the original. Self-taught, Mr. Rundell has instructed others, including Mary L. Tilley, whose work appears in figure 68. His initials are seen carved inside the middle handle. O.H. 13¼"; L. 25"; W. 17¾".

Achieving beauty can be a deliberate function of basketry, as it is with open-sided baskets, such as that of plate 3, and those with the more common scalloped edge. These were regularly depicted in still-life paintings or drawings. One collector called hers a "theorem basket" because she was reminded of those in old schoolgirl art projects, and baskets have caught the fancy of needleworkers, too (fig. 6).

There are practices that have been devised to increase a basket's longevity, other than the logical ones of tight weaving and obtaining good materials. A set of outer splints, called heels, runners, drags, or cleats, may be added on to buffer the bottom during heavy use. While wooden bases (pl. 4) lend strength—the bottom can't break through when pierced or overloaded, as individual weavers might do—they also add considerably to a basket's weight.

A burden may be distributed by providing a pair of handles, one at each end, so two people can share the carrying. A three-handled

FIGURE 13. Rib-type baskets of round rods. (Left) The "corrugated" lines of this willow basket, which must be of fairly recent date, indicate Minnesota Chippewa manufacture. (Center) The small squashed shape (tilted forward) was found in New England and reminds me of examples photographed at a Washington, D.C., rural handicrafts exhibition in 1937. (Right) A new Appalachian honeysuckle vine "Betty basket," so nicknamed by a dealer who was reluctant to divulge the full name of her Kentucky source. The basket incorporates hickory hoops and inner bark (for the "diamonds" or "folded squares" at the joins) and dogwood twigs for ribs. O.H. 12½".

version, suited either for a light load held with one hand or for two-handed transport, may be studied in figure 12.

European-born craftworkers, many from the British Isles, introduced the more difficult but stout rib-type construction (fig. 13) to native basketmakers, and some eastern tribes adopted it into their repertoire. To begin such a basket, rim and handle hoops are tied together at right angles, then the ribs are forced into the joins to complete a skeleton into which weavers are introduced.

Although few folk artisans may be expected to have heard the "form follows function" dictum proclaimed by skyscraper architect Louis Sullivan, the good ones work by it, both intuitively and consciously. Among significant examples of purely functional basketry that will be scattered throughout subsequent chapters is the Afro-American rice fanner in plate 14, a simple winnower that meets the requirements of this type of agricultural tool: ruggedness, large surface area combined with shallow depth, and lightness of weight.

NATIVE PEOPLES

While most people with a serious interest in Amerind craft arts are well aware of the incredible assortment of baskets made by the original inhabitants of the Western Hemisphere, the majority evinces wonder if not disbelief at hearing that there really are over fifty North American Indian tribes still producing baskets. Admittedly, in a great many situations, including groups once famous for their basketry, there may be left mere pockets of survival or only one or a tiny band of active basketmakers in the entire tribe, and these are elderly women with a slight output that is possibly only enough for themselves, as there are no apprentices to train. It should not be unexpected that comparatively few utility forms persist or that the bulk of quality production is eagerly sought by collectors, while much of the rest that is turned out is aimed at the relatively unsophisticated tourist buyers who are willing to pay only souvenir prices.

During the past several years I have been making special efforts to collect from a number of tribes I hadn't visited previously and include the results in this chapter. Many remain to be seen. Research through fieldwork is almost invariably necessary, and I plan to contact additional tribes on their home grounds as time permits and travel facilitates this study. (Let me slip in the suggestion that a visitor on Indian lands would be well advised to keep in mind that he or she is a guest there and that, for the majority of traditional Native Americans who live on reservations, English is a second language. A few communities are even closed to outsiders, as is conservative Old Oraibi, Arizona, said to have been occupied continuously since the twelfth century.)

What follows is a compendium of Indian-American basketry structured according to a geographic breakdown, as, in most instances, a given climate and physical resources would give rise to a general material culture in which related or parallel groups made similar goods.

NORTHWEST PACIFIC COAST

Chicago's Field Museum of Natural History mounted a memorable three-month exhibition, beginning December 15, 1977, "Basketry of the Northwest Coast Indians," one hundred basketry items from the collections, most of them acquired around 1900. There were thirteen cases holding a great selection, everything from cradles to watertight drinking cups, berrying baskets, and storage trunks. Each case had a theme, say, "Acorn Gathering and Processing," and there were samples of materials and tools, as well as photographs. The low-key design of the installation was just right, and the particularly well-written explanations led even casual visitors to consider possible reasons for the extreme diversity of forms, functions, and techniques (richness of plant life, population density and ensuing competition over natural resources, lingering premigration influences, and so on).

Two days of demonstrations brought Karok craftswomen from northwestern California, and I was able to purchase two new twined pieces, an openwork willow-twig burden basket and a woman's dress head cap (fig. 14). Their maker had been chosen to be medicine woman (as she put it, what white society might call "queen") for the major annual event, the festival for the New Year coming in August; she was to appear in full costume, wearing a hat resembling that shown and carrying such a basket.

The three principal basketmaking tribes of northern California are (from north to south) the Karok, Yurok, and Hupa, neighbors who share a river (the Klamath) and closely resemblant customs. An

FIGURE 14. Karok (northwestern California) twined basketry, a burden basket and woman's dress head cap/hat: collected from their maker, Madeline Davis of Happy Camp, during a Field Museum (Chicago) demonstration in early 1978. (Right) All willow, except rim bound with bear grass, a bunch grass that is bleached in the sun to "get white"; the flattened side is worn against the back suspended from a tumpline (head strap). H. 9½"; Rim 9½" x 8". (Left) Ribs of hazel twigs (they can be willow), foundation split pine root, overlaid, in a simultaneous weaving, with pale bear grass and shiny black maidenhair fern and brown sword fern stems (this last dyed with alder bark). H. 4"; Diam. 8".

FIGURE 15. Twined woman's dress head cap/hat that is probably Hupa (northwestern California): early twentieth century. A number of western tribes twined hats, some plain ones to protect the forehead from rubbing by a carrying strap. Work caps fit close to the head, whereas dress caps touched only at the rim. Widows wore undecorated caps, and the men of the Hupa, Karok, and Yurok also had plain hats that doubled as tobacco scoops. The encircling band of stepped or terraced lines with triangles is false embroidery, that is, the design doesn't show on the inside because it is nipped in on the outer surface only. H. 3″; Diam. 6¾″.

old Hupa hat is illustrated in figure 15, succeeded by an Edward S. Curtis photograph of the imposing principal shaman of the Hupa, a woman who is obviously the repository of great medicine, wearing one (fig. 16). (Plain caps were also worn by many western tribespeople to protect the forehead from chafing by burden basket tumplines, carrying straps that were themselves of vegetal material. Other types of basketry head coverings included big hats that were the umbrellas of the rainy Northwest Coast.)

The work of Edward Sheriff (his mother's English maiden name) Curtis, photographer, self-taught ethnographer, cinematographer, lecturer, writer, and a man of prodigious talents but a bare grammar

FIGURE 16. "Principal Female Shaman of the Hupa," photographed by Edward S. Curtis: published in 1923 as plate 467 in the portfolio to volume 13 of Curtis's *The North American Indian* series. His caption read in part: "Many Hupa shamans were women, and, among their neighbors, the Yurok and the Karok, as well as among the more distant Wiyot on the coast, male shamans were rare. Hupa shamans acquired the power to cure disease by dreaming and dancing." To an ailing patient, the mere sight of this powerful face at bedside must have been a great comfort if not a restorative. Among these tribes, the twined cap was a topping essential to complete a woman's traditional costume. With some, designs invented by a medicine woman were respected as her exclusive property, and none dared copy them for fear of retaliation through her presumed or experienced "ability to inflict mysterious sickness by sorcery." Photograph courtesy Boston Public Library, Department of Rare Books & Manuscripts, Boston, Massachusetts, and by permission Florence Curtis Graybill.

FIGURE 17. Makah (Washington) ornamental basket, a trinket basket; cedar bark and grass in wrapped-twine technique, with motifs in false embroidery using aniline colors of purple, red, green, bright pink, and black: modern. The mirror shows the opposite side, where whalers in an open boat chase their quarry around the basket. I've seen a similar little basket, purchased in Vancouver, that had been made by the Nootka of British Columbia. The Makah are a division of the Nootka, and whaling was formerly the very dangerous chief occupation of the men in both. A Makah or Nootka basket (museums don't always differentiate between the two, and the best of them are incredibly fine of weave) in an Indian arts dealer's advertisement had one of the leviathans in the process of swallowing a manned boat. H. and Diam. 1½".

school education, has returned to the public eye. With a consuming urgency to record traditional American Indian life before it had completely faded from sight or living memory, with Teddy Roosevelt's good wishes, and with some of J. Pierpont Morgan's money, Curtis began his fieldwork as a vigorous man in his thirties and concluded it three decades later, exhausted and suffering from physical and economic hardships that left him with a thin wallet and ailments like a permanently damaged hip, which he suffered when a whale capsized his boat during a filming episode. He wrote, illustrated, and published the twenty-volume opus that he called simply *The North American Indian*, which was accompanied by portfolios of large separate plates, for a total of 2,200 photographs in the entire set.

To raise the rest of the funding for the project, Curtis sold advance subscriptions and individual prints, borrowed from friends, became a filmmaker, and took to the lecture circuit. With a four-horse wagon to move his bulky equipment, he crisscrossed the western part of the continent, starting with the Southwest, running through the Plains, into the Northwest, down the Pacific Coast, and capped his work with a study of the Eskimo. He achieved acceptance by many

FIGURE 18. "Waiting for the Canoe" (Nootka), photographed by Edward S. Curtis: published in 1915 as plate 387 in the portfolio to volume 11 of *The North American Indian* series. His caption was: "As evening approaches, two women with clam baskets and digging sticks gaze across the water, anxiously awaiting the canoe that is to come and convey them home." While this picture was taken on Nootka Island off the western shore of Vancouver Island, British Columbia, it shows the kind of utility baskets and cedar-bark (the supple inner bark) garments that would have been prevalent among the Makah of Washington's Olympic Peninsula. They are a Nootka tribe with a similar maritime economy and could as easily have been the subjects. One woman supports her burden basket by means of a tumpline (the strap passing across her head). Photograph courtesy Boston Public Library, Department of Rare Books & Manuscripts, Boston, Massachusetts.

tribes as few trained anthropologists have been able to do, even to winning eventual participation in the Hopi Snake Dance. Much of his photography had to be of painstakingly planned and posed reconstructions.[3] A 1975 film biography aptly titles Curtis "The Shadow Catcher."

The Makah, a division of the Nootka, have settled at the farthest northwest portion of Washington, which is a promontory that has the Pacific Ocean against its western length and juts northward into Juan de Fuca Strait. They weave a modest amount for their own use but twined ornamental baskets are mostly made for sale (see fig. 17 for a wee one that portrays a whale hunt). In earlier days they would have had utility baskets like those in the Curtis photograph of two Nootka women, dressed in cedar-bark garments, who have been gathering clams (fig. 18).

Even though a few other small tribal groups in the region are said to produce a minor measure of basketry, I have never been offered any of their new pieces.

SOUTHWEST

As a function of its size, extended latitudinal orientation, and wide range of altitudes, California incorporates several kinds of environments, each of which hosted an indigenous culture adapted to it. This was also the most heavily populated tract of what later became the United States. Ethnologist A. L. Kroeber devoted a lifetime to research and his writings about the original Californians; his *Handbook of the Indians of California* (1925, 1976) is a classic reference.

While in the northernmost zone there evolved the affluent salmon-fishing civilization akin to that of coastal dwellers in the territory that became the State of Washington and the Canadian Province of British Columbia, central California was inhabited by groups who depended largely upon wild-growing plant foods. Acorns have been eaten by over half our tribes, with the Southwestern Pomo having consumed around a pound per family per day; they are still a significant dietary element at some settlements, especially in times of economic adversity.[4] The Pomo ground the acorns into flour that had to be filtered several times to leach out the poisonous tannin, then turned it into their staple—acorn mush or gruel—which was boiled by throwing hot stones into a tightly twined basket holding water and the meal. Their craft was basketry, and what baskets they wrought!

Tribeswomen twined all sorts of utilitarian and fine cooking baskets but were acclaimed principally for their feather-covered coiled treasure baskets (a museum-quality specimen glows from pl. 5). When Sir Francis Drake saw these baskets on the West Coast in 1579, their surpassing beauty brought forth his admiration, and his chronicles reported "matted down of red feathers, distinguished into divers workes and formes" [motifs].

Feathers were worked onto the outer surface in patterns of two or three colors as a gently flaring bowl was coiled. It was often embellished with shell decorations, and a strap was attached from which the beautiful thing could be hung proudly in the home. These important baskets were mainly gifts upon great occasions: a woman might make her future son-in-law such a basket and present it to him

FIGURE 19. Pomo (central California) partially feathered basket, three-rod willow foundation bound with sedge root and arrowhead elements in black-stained bulrush root: c. 1915. The sparse tufts of small red-orange feathers woven onto the light background are from a locally available species of woodpecker. The shape is referred to as a "canoe"; a much larger one in the Field Museum of Natural History's extensive Pomo collection is identified as a medicine man's, used for storing ritual paraphernalia. Many of the oval or round baskets were ornamented with beads of shell or glass and some with quail head plumes. H. ¾"; L. 5¼"; W. 3".

at the wedding; it was usually cremated with him in death. Always highly esteemed and extremely valuable, these baskets can rarely be acquired nowadays, and only a few small ones have been finished in recent years.

A more affordable acquisition, albeit far more modest, was the partially feathered (with small tufts of red-orange fluff from a local woodpecker), canoe-shaped shallow basket of figure 19. The Field Museum has a comprehensive permanent display of Pomo basketry that includes eight or nine coiled baskets similarly sparsely decorated with like bits of the identical feathers.

Her name was first *Dabuda* (Young Willow), and from 1888 she was Louisa Keyser (her married name). But the impressive Datsolalee (the spelling varies), a Washo, is remembered by the Indian name of her maturity, which has been translated as versions of "Wide Hips" and "Broad-in-the-Hips." Figure 20 is her portrait. In her own time and since Datsolalee has been the most celebrated American basketmaker, partly because she early on gained good public relations in the active person of merchant Abe Cohn, in whose childhood home she had once done housework and who was proprietor of the Emporium in Carson City, Nevada. He became her patron and was for thirty years her business manager and exclusive agent, even settling his temperamental protégée and her second husband Charley in a little frame house next to his, and finally assuring fairly uninterrupted production from her by promising to provide food, clothes, and to meet all their other needs as long as they lived.

Datsolalee was a huge, emotional woman accustomed to having her own way and given to bouts of temper or tearful outbursts. It once happened that, while irate with Charley for having managed to land behind bars to serve out a jail term, she started a wildly irregular basket ("My Mad Basket"). When the marital skies cleared with his release and her bestowal of forgiveness, she finished the basket with her customary careful execution. Such anecdotes about Datsolalee and Mr. Cohn's caretaking make lively reading in Jane Green Gigli's "Dat So La Lee, Queen of the Washo Basket Makers." [5]

FIGURE 20. Portrait of Datsolalee, a Washo Indian world-renowned basketmaker: photographed by Mrs. Abe Cohn, wife of her exclusive agent, in Carson City, Nevada, 1897. Although her birth year is not certain, Datsolalee's life-span is usually given as 1831 to 1925. The looped stick (*baleo*) is a tong for handling hot stones when boiling mush in a basket and sometimes for stirring, but we can't know why one is prominent in the picture. (The small pedestal is an unfortunate prop that crops up in basket photographs of the period.) Photograph courtesy Nevada State Museum, Carson City, Nevada.

FIGURE 21. Basket masterpiece by Datsolalee, a Washo; white mountain-willow twigs with motifs in black bracken fern stems and reddish-brown bark of the redbud tree: begun March 26, 1917, finished February 16, 1918, and documented by agent Abe Cohn as number LK 61. Whereas a *degikup* (refers to the spherical, small-mouthed shape) was ordinarily a food bowl, quality examples would have been intended strictly for ceremonial purposes. Datsolalee's pieces were recognized as works of art. Referred to by one expert (Coe, see Selected Bibliography) as "the summation of her work," this basket's beautifully controlled, swelling line and proportions are in harmonious concert with the rhythmic flame motifs, which appear regularly in her work; it coalesces the highest artistic realization with complete mastery of technical skills. Its size, over 51″ in circumference, and taut weave demanded more than 30 stitches to the inch, over 100,000 altogether. Surprisingly, it was completed not long before the onset of blindness. When questioned, Datsolalee gave the meaning of the design as: "We assemble to discuss the happy lives of our ancestors." H. 12″; Max. diam. 16¼″; Min. diam. 7¾″. Photograph courtesy the Clark Field Collection, Philbrook Art Center, Tulsa, Oklahoma.

Figure 21 has the particular globular basket that has received the most attention and that may well be considered her greatest masterpiece, but it almost has to be seen in the fiber (it was in the "Sacred Circles" show at the Nelson Gallery of Art—Atkins Museum of Fine Arts in Kansas City, Missouri, 1977) in order to grasp its monumental quality. Somehow, the basket looms even bigger than it actually is; it is a work of vast restraint and refinement.

Mr. Cohn meticulously catalogued significant pieces as they came from Datsolalee's beringed and diminutive hands, so we know he numbered and sold 121, 46 of them major (i.e. large-scale) items. The fineness and sheer bulk of her pieces called for laborious preparation of quantities of several materials, yet her tool for this was a shard of glass with which to cut and smooth.

A substantial collection of Datsolalee's art (it should be mentioned that there were several other recognized Washo craftswomen), including miniatures, utilitarian trays, and mush bowls, is at the Nevada State Museum in Carson City. Rather a body of literature has been published about the legendary basketmaker, including an analysis that traces the stylistic development of the corpus of her work.[6]

At a 1971 Sotheby Parke Bernet auction of the Green Collection, composed of six Datsolalee baskets, prices ranged from $2,800 to $6,100, for an average of almost $4,400. They would doubtless bring considerably more today; her very finest might carry valuations well up into five figures. During her lifetime, Datsolalee's best baskets could bring thousands of dollars apiece, and one collector paid $5,000 (I believe for that basket in fig. 21).

The Chemehuevi—originally Californian but now living in Arizona—whose coiled basketry was influenced by contact with the surrounding indigenous cultures in California, the Great Basin, and the Southwest, no longer produce. Birdie H. Brown, a prominent collector of the tribe's work fifty years ago, clutches her latest and beams at us from figure 22. Three vendors have set out quite an assortment of baskets. The subtle basket in the hands of the woman at the right exhibits Chemehuevi design at its elegant best (said to possess an

FIGURE 22. The collector (Birdie H. Brown) and her Chemehuevi suppliers (Alice Waco, Annie Laird, and Mary Snyder): c. 1930. Most of the small, formerly seminomadic tribe who lived in the eastern portion of California's Mojave Desert moved to the Colorado River Reservation, Parker, Arizona. They made excellent coiled baskets of willow with desgns in devil's-claw (*Martynia louisianica*). Although basketry was their major craft, it is no longer produced. Photograph courtesy The Fred Harvey Fine Arts Collection, Heard Museum, Phoenix, Arizona.

"almost oriental sensibility" by curator Ralph T. Coe, see Selected Bibliography).

Where pueblo potters coiled huge grain-storage jars, sedentary desert tribes devised granaries of plant fibers. One found in museums is the Piman type; some had great capacity, as does that of figure 23, whose maker sits inside it as she coils along.

The Piman tongue is also spoken by the Papago, who inhabit an immense reservation in southern Arizona and are the most prolific basketmakers of all, with perhaps two thousand engaged in some stage of basketmaking. Both tribes made, with minor differences, the same coiled-willow baskets; a turn-of-the-century Pima tray/bowl with a whirlwind sweeping from center to rim may be studied in figure 24.

FIGURE 23. Pima (Arizona) woman sitting inside a huge, partially finished granary basket as she works: this picture appeared in a book published in 1916. The wheat-straw foundation bundle could be an inch or more in diameter, with an inch or more between stitches of mesquite bark or willow. These crude baskets, with capacities of up to fifty bushels, stored wheat in the home. The soft straw was quite vulnerable to rodents, and, in fact, one photograph I've seen contains the meaningful detail of a kitten playing alongside. Photograph courtesy Heard Museum, Phoenix, Arizona.

FIGURE 24. Turn-of-the-century Pima (Arizona) tray/shallow bowl, willow, with whirling design in devil's-claw. The rotational symmetry of the four-armed design is also exhibited in work by the closely related Papago, both "Old Papago" of willow and the modern yucca (see bowl at right foreground in fig. 25). However, the Papago tended to weave their willow baskets with flatter bases and they are somewhat heavier and less flexible. Antique Pima baskets are much in demand, as are the very few being produced today, those mostly by women who are mixed Pima and Papago. For their new baskets, the clue to tribal identification lies with the material: willow makes it Pima and yucca makes it Papago. H. 2¾"; Diam. 9".

As willow became scarce on the dry Papago lands and in order to turn out a basket in less time so they could meet vacationers' requests to sell cheaply, their weavers switched to yucca in the early twentieth century and began to coil a new kind of basket in which much of the bear-grass foundation was left exposed and the yucca-splint binding was sewn with an open split stitch. Figure 25 contains two baskets of this modern type and three in which the core material is completely covered over. Where motifs are in the dark devil's-claw (*Martynia louisianica*), which is harder to obtain, prepare, and work with (it is sometimes dyed black to get an even color, as different parts of the pod may vary in intensity from black to gray), a basket costs roughly twice as much as does its equivalent bound entirely with yucca.

Artisans employing willow, less than a dozen of them doing so regularly, are mostly mixed Pima and Papago living in the Chuichu area at the extreme northern tip of the Papago Reservation, not far from the Pimas' Gila River Reservation. The last-named tribe owns an

FIGURE 25. Papago (Arizona) yucca baskets, a "recent" commercial adaptation; bear-grass foundation bound with yucca leaf, some with motifs in devil's-claw: 1977. The flat plaque with the Man-in-the-Maze, called Elder Brother (who built his house within a labyrinth of trails to confuse his enemies), is 14″ across. (Left) Two excellent examples of the contemporary type, showing exposed cores sewn in split stitch. (The *olla* [jar] was made in two pieces.) Others on the market have the coils completely cast over with yucca and designs worked out with green, sun-bleached yellow, or white leaves. (Right) Ants. (Next) Carefully executed swirl of tight, narrow coils by a woman known only by sight to a trader at Sells, from whom it was bought for $100. From various makers, all were purchased among three of the more accessible trading posts on the Papago Reservation, each of which has a separate "basket room"; the bundle of yucca splints cost 75¢. (The Navajo textile is in a Wide Ruins pattern of Ganado Red-dyed and natural wools.)

FIGURE 26. Coiled miniatures from Arizona tribes: 1976–1977. (Left) Pima and Papago group of natural horsehair from tails or manes, sewn with horsehair or thread. (Clockwise) Pima (many weavers are part-Papago and may live on that reservation) willow-and-devil's-claw. The lizard basket is by Martha Manuel. The purple-ribboned tray (diam. slightly more than 4″) with the three-petal squash blossom took the prize for Gladys Antone at the Inter-Tribal Indian Ceremonial at Gallup, New Mexico, 1976, where she captured a second prize for a larger basket; she has taught two daughters. Willow oval with recumbent deer (?). Eleven-coil Hopi deep basket with kachina head.

excellent arts and crafts shop at Sacaton that stocks baskets and other handcrafts by Indian Americans in Arizona and New Mexico.

The Pima and Papago do miniatures, some of horsehair and others of willow or yucca (fig. 26). It is a fact that miniature baskets have been recovered from numerous Southwestern archaeological sites; [7] and their purposes have been much speculated about but seldom determined.

Basketry of the Papago and Pima Indians by Mary Lois Kissell (1916, 1972) gives as figure 44 helpful drawings of "Forms of Papago and Pima Bowls and Trays."

Least influenced by Anglo contacts are the Hopi. Some say that there are really three Hopi tribes, not one, because the culture differs from one to another of their three northern Arizona mesas, and that, therefore, the Hopi should be dealt with as three separate political entities. Figure 26 includes a Hopi coiled miniature with kachina-head motif; there are hundreds of kachinas (deified ancestral spirits),

FIGURE 27. Western Apache (Arizona) twined basketry; materials are customarily split willow, young squawberry bush, or wild mulberry: 1976–1977. (Left) Burden basket, a 2½″ model, complete to buckskin-reinforced bottom and fringes tipped with metals cones that tinkle when the basket is moved, as they did when big ones were carried on women's backs. Collection of Mr. and Mrs. John H. Luckner. (Right) Small *tus* or water bottle/jar/canteen with twig handles through which to pass a strap, from Cibecue on the Fort Apache Reservation. It has been smeared with red ocher clay. Before actual use, large baskets for the transport (often from long distances) and storage of water would have been thoroughly waterproofed, first by filling the interstices with ground leaves and/or clay and then by applying a thick coating of warmed piñon pine pitch.

FIGURE 28. Bottle believed to be of Paiute manufacture, and most likely for storing seeds or nuts, made by the twining method: early twentieth century(?). Large pointed-bottom jars were also made by others, among them the Apache, Havasupai, Walapai, and prehistoric peoples in the Southwest, but they were ordinarily for hauling and keeping precious water and would have been coated with pitch. The pointed base prevented the total loss of the contents if the container was dropped. H. 11"; W. 6½". Photograph by Helga Photo Studio, New York.

some unique to the villages of a particular mesa, and their depictions are frequent in Hopi basketry. Other examples are presented in plate 6 in both coiled and wickerwork methods with representational or geometric designs. Coiling is done exclusively on Second Mesa (once called Middle Mesa) and decorative wickerwork only on Third Mesa (West Mesa), although plaited and wickerwork utility baskets may be made in every Hopi town.

The Western Apache (Arizona) were famous for what has been called San Carlos–type coiled basketry, but there is little production of the type now. Quite a bit of twined basketry is sold, though. A flat-bottomed *tus* or water jar from Cibecue on the Fort Apache Reservation and a miniature of the once-ubiquitous fringed burden basket appear in figure 27.

A twined bottle shape believed to have been intended for seeds or nuts and of probable Paiute origin is pictured (fig. 28). Tightly woven, pointed-bottom forms have been resin-pitched to supply ancient and historic groups in the arid domain with water holders and carriers.

Clara Lee Tanner's *Prehistoric Southwestern Craft Arts* (1976) has a scholarly chapter on pottery that considers the pervasive "basket influence," particularly noticeable in the oldest ceramic finds, over vessel shapes, as well as the geometric and angular treatment evidenced in ancient decoration.

SOUTH-CENTRAL REGION

The Cherokee of Oklahoma are descended from those who were re-settled through the "Trail of Tears" from the Great Smoky Mountains

FIGURE 29.   Cherokee of Oklahoma buckbrush basket of modern design usual with them: 1975. Whereas most forms are more contemporary than those of the Eastern Band of Cherokee (North Carolina), this basket without the handle would be equivalent to the last-named's fruit basket of wild honeysuckle vine. The Oklahoma buckbrush runners are colored with synthetics, but the North Carolinians prepare dyes from their region's plants. O.H. 7¾"; Diam. 6½".

FIGURE 30. Canework from the Alabama-Coushatta Reservation (eastern Texas) by Maggie Poncho, a venerable pure Alabama: 1975. The shiny outer skin of the cane shows on the outsides of baskets. The hominy sieve/ corn flour sifter (rear, 13″) is shaken while held over a twilled tray (at left, also called a fanner) and retains the coarse particles. The high-handled basket is a small version of a type given as a present and was to be hung over one's arm; the other, a wall basket, was a gift the weaver included with the three ordered. Only one other woman, who lives in the area but off the reservation, still weaves with cane. Getting the material and preparing it has proved to be such an obstacle that competitors have found it simpler to do pine-needle baskets.

of North Carolina almost one hundred and fifty years ago. They sell buckbrush-runner baskets of modern design with synthetic colors (fig. 29) from their shop at Tahlequah.

A number of tribal agencies have formed craftsmen's marketing organizations, often with retail stores, on reservation lands. Such shops normally handle quality goods at fair prices and provide a convenient way to obtain items that may prove difficult or impossible to get otherwise.

Purchasing directly from an artisan almost invariably demands time and effort but can be personally rewarding, as it was when I met the lovely, aged lady who plaited the cane baskets in figure 30 on the Alabama-Coushatta Reservation (near Livingston) in eastern Texas.

A coiled basket from the tribal shop at the same reservation is in figure 31, along with others by the Koasati of Elton, Louisiana. They are popularly known as Coushatta and have a retail sales outlet at the Cultural Center in Elton, where a uniquely shaped basket was also bought (pl. 7). Both groups make miniatures, photographed in figure 32.

FIGURE 31. Coiled baskets by related tribal groups of Louisiana and Texas: all collected new in their locales in 1975. (Foreground) Koasati (Coushatta of Louisiana) medicine basket, Spanish moss with blue beads (a curator said it would be filled with herbs for a healing ceremony and buried at its conclusion). (Left rear) Koasati shallow covered bowl, brown pine needles bound with raffia in decorative wheat-stitch, in which an extra stitch is placed to the side of each split stitch. (Right rear) From the Alabama-Coushatta Reservation in east Texas, a small covered pot of dry pine needles bound with raffia in plain split stitch. All these baskets are in the natural colors of the materials, although dyed imported raffia is employed for bindings on some. Largest, H. 2¾"; Diam. 6½".

FIGURE 32. Coiled miniatures from the Koasati (Louisiana) and the Alabama-Coushatta Reservation (eastern Texas), pine needles and raffia: 1975. (Left) Bought in the shop at the Alabama-Coushatta Reservation near Livingston, Texas. H. 1″; L. 2¼″; W. 2″. (Right) Made by a full-blooded Alabama, purchased in the Coushatta Cultural Center's shop at Elton, Louisiana. H. 1¾″; Diam. 2″.

FIGURE 33. Eastern Band of Choctaws (Mississippi) plaited baskets, swamp cane, synthetic dyes: 1975. (Left) Colorful sewing basket with different patterning on lid and sides; by Jeffie Solomon. Bottom 8″ sq.; Diam. 10¼″. (Right) Doublewoven deep basket by Susan Denson; this technique involves the simultaneous weaving of one basket inside another so that there is a different pattern inside and out. H. 8¼″; Diam. 7″. Acquired through the Choctaw Craft Association at Philadelphia, Mississippi.

FIGURE 34. Choctaw (Mississippi) miniatures, swamp cane: 1975. The two in the middle are meant to be hung. Largest, O.H. 4″; Diam. 2½″.

The Eastern or Mississippi Band of Choctaws sells swamp-cane baskets (pl. 8, fig. 33) at the Choctaw Craft Association at Philadelphia. Figure 34 has Choctaw cane miniatures.

SOUTHEAST

Going west into the Florida Everglades on the Tamiami Trail (U.S. 41) out of Miami, I went in and out of countless demonstration Indian villages until I'd bagged the two attractive and well-made Seminole coiled-grass, cotton-stitched, lidded baskets shown in figure 35, along with one by the closely related (both are Creek) Miccosukee tribe. The last-named have a nice arts and crafts shop just opposite

FIGURE 35. Seminole and Miccosukee (Florida) coiled baskets, made in the Everglades swamps: 1977. The base is started with a circle of brown palmetto fiber, to which grass coils are stitched with colored cotton thread, several colors to each basket. The Miccosukee basket (farthest left) is H. 7¼″; Diam. 7½″. (An expert, commenting upon the close resemblance of its outline to that of the in-and-out basket in pl. 14, has a theory that its maker may have seen similar Afro-Carolinian pieces.) Both the others are Seminole; the larger is 7½″ across.

the entrance to the National Park Service's Shark Valley Tramway, where the Seminole corn-grinding baskets (fig. 36) I'd almost despaired of getting were hanging on the wall. Although the type may be found in use among traditional families, they're an elusive quarry for the collector.

FIGURE 36. Seminole plaited corn-grinding set consisting of sieve, which is suspended here, and tray; palmetto splints: purchased unused in Florida in 1977. These were not made as a set, only assembled as one. The sieve is held in one hand as ground corn is poured in, then the second hand taps the sieve so that the sifted flour falls through into the tray that is sitting below. Such baskets may be found in use in Everglades homes, but they're seldom available through conventional sources. The tray's twilled weave clearly shows the diagonal effect: H. 3"; 16" sq. Sieve, H. 1½"; 13½" sq. (See fig. 30 for similar baskets in cane collected on the Alabama-Coushatta Reservation [eastern Texas]; the Iroquois also had sieves, theirs in black-ash splint.)

Before European contact, our indigenous peoples utilized basketry fibers and techniques to shelter and clothe themselves, and almost all made mats for sleeping and eating on. Long out of use, they linger only in museum exhibits. (In remote parts of Mexico, a tule *petate* may still serve as the poor man's bed.) However, the

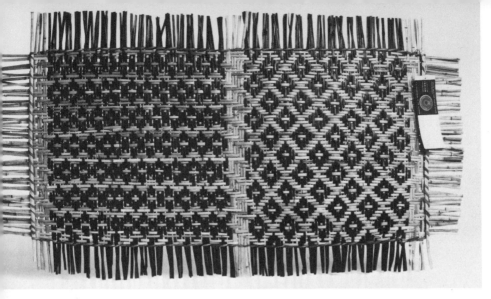

FIGURE 37. Twilled wall mat from the Eastern Band of Cherokee (North Carolina), river cane with butternut-root dye, by Lucy G. Long: purchased for $75 in 1974 through the Qualla Arts & Crafts Mutual, Inc., at Cherokee. Distinguished by being worked in two variations of an allover geometric pattern called Chief's Daughters. Although these mats are considered to be decorative pieces to hang on the wall, almost all tribes east of the Great Plains once had floor mats in their lodges on which the family sat, ate, and slept. Some groups lived in shelters built as frameworks that were covered with waterproof mats lashed over walls and ceiling, and mats formed partitions in bigger dwellings. They were put to countless other uses. L. 39"; W. 21."

Eastern Band of Cherokee in North Carolina turn out cane mats that are meant to be displayed as wall decoration (fig. 37).

The tribe continues a healthy basketmaking industry. Their basket prices keep going up, but they're selling well. More younger weavers are at work, with the youngest member of the Qualla Arts & Crafts Mutual on the reservation at Cherokee eighteen years old, and little girls of four and five busy trying to help make splints for their mothers (basketry is practiced almost solely by women). Three materials—river cane, white oak, and wild honeysuckle vine—are employed. Dyes are brewed from roots and such, the many basket types remain much as they were when I toured in 1974, and several exhibitions featuring individual basketmakers have been held since.

NORTHEAST

Ted J. Brasser's *A Basketful of Indian Culture Change* (1975) presents the case that wood-splint plaiting was introduced into New England by Swedish colonists around 1700 and taken up by local Indians. Later, it provided a marginal living for those who had lost their former means of livelihood, so that a Seneca orator of the 1760s warned against Christianity, lest his people be setting foot on the path to basketmak-

FIGURE 38. Wide-splint baskets with "potato"-type design stampings formerly common among Algonkians and Iroquoians, black ash: most probably around 100 years old. Motifs carved out of pieces of potato, turnip, or wood were dipped into vegetal dyes and pressed against wide splints. Indian-invented devices that produced narrow splints efficiently ended this decorative method. Farther back, designs had been hand painted. (Center foreground) Bobbin basket with stepped backplate was hung on loom posts; known as comb baskets among eastern tribespeople, who propped a mirror against the back and kept small personal items in the trough. H. and L. approx. 7½". This and the 16"-diameter basket (left rear) have some colored splints. The bonnet basket/hatbox/bandbox served white New Englanders as travel luggage and protected clothing at home; they were fitted with chintz covers. (Left) Rectangular storage basket; most were substantially larger. (Right) Handled basket with sloping shoulder identifying Indian workmanship.

FIGURE 39. Centenarian "Penobscot" basket, black ash. Black and red colors painted onto the outsides of the standards or ribs were used to achieve an animallike striping that is particularly lovely against the patina of the natural wood, now aged to nut brown. Known for their skillful construction, strength, and vigor of design and color, old Penobscot baskets, of which a good collection is at the Robert Abbe Museum of Stone Age Antiquities in Acadia National Park near Bar Harbor, Maine, may well rank first among New England Indian work. The tribe's name came to be a genre name for top-quality decorated baskets in Maine. It would be difficult to equal the distinction of this one, which is also perfectly preserved, a rare occurrence at this age. O.H. 8"; Diam. 13".

FIGURE 41. Mohawk (New York State) decorated baskets, black ash and sweet grass, some braided: 1977. Largest, Diam. 12". Most collected at Akwesasne, the Mohawk name for the St. Regis Reservation, part of which is in Canada. The three large covered baskets are in the natural colors of the wood and grass, while the brightly tinted splints incorporated into the others were dyed with synthetics. The great bulk of production among the Iroquois Nations is Mohawk. (Right rear) Made by Mary Adams, whom several named as the best active weaver among them; she has been making baskets more than fifty years. A top view of the small cone-shaped basket at far right shows on the front cover, where it rests on its side at the left end of the crock stand's center shelf.

FIGURE 40. Old fine-splint Indian baskets from the Northeast, black ash. (Left) Acorn-shaped basket that came with a Shaker attribution but resembles, in its tapering lines and proportions, Indian-made baskets, including a Wampanoag in a museum collection. O.H. 10¾"; Diam. 7". (Rear) Open sewing/workbasket with four hexagonal-weave side trays, pockets attached inside just under the rim, allover porcupine-curlicue decoration, and twilled bottom. The shape is said to be a Maine specialty, but it is also reminiscent of a burden basket being woven by one woman among the Cherokee of North Carolina. H. 5¼"; Rim diam. 12½"; Base 5" sq. (Right foreground) Sweet-grass-covered miniature with faded salmon pink splints; a middle-aged Mohawk woman showed me similar heirlooms from her childhood. H. less than 1"; Diam .2½".

FIGURE 42. Toy crib for a doll, a hooded bed of natural black-ash splint with curlicue decoration, a band of sweet grass around the rim, and little supporting feet of splint curls (others have rockers). H. 5¾"; L. 9½"; W. 5". These, made by the Mohawks of New York State, come in several sizes. The Passamaquoddy tribe of Maine have made a 28"-long model mounted on a high cradle stand and meant for a real baby.

ing pauperdom. (Mr. Brasser located this reference in the Sam Kirkland Papers at Hamilton College, Clinton, New York.)

Figures 38 through 40 present antique ash-splint baskets: four with "potato"-type design stampings, a "Penobscot," and a miscellaneous grouping; the captions contain fuller information. As to current manufacture, the Passamaquoddy tribe of Maine, who produce a quantity of both decorative and utilitarian baskets, had disbanded their basket cooperative and its stores by 1977. A prospective buyer

FIGURE 43. Iroquois utilitarian baskets, all Mohawk-made: 1976–1977. (Left) Corn washer/corn-hulling/corn-soup basket with twilled-weave sides and simple-plaited openwork bottom. The text explains its application. Still found in the kitchens of Iroquois communities, the weaver has one for her own cooking. H. 8½″; Diam. 11″. (Rear) Gathering basket of black-ash splint with handhold openings under the rim. I believe this one is Canadian, but I saw them sold at Iroquois locations in New York State, there called laundry baskets. H. 10″; L. 25″; W. 17″. (Right) Salt storage bottle of braided cornhusk strips sewn with white cotton thread, cob stopper; copy of an old form long out of use. H. and Diam. 6″. Also of braided cornhusks are Huskface Society masks, whose male wearers officiate at planting and harvest celebrations or ritual healings; here is one marked "guardian size."

might try going into one of their locations, Pleasant Point in Perry and Peter Dana Point, Indian Township, near Princeton. The Penobscots, who once had such a reputation for fine decorated baskets that theirs became a genre name for the best Maine baskets, do offer some on Indian Island, Old Town (north of Bangor).

A 1977 field trip onto several Iroquois (the Six Nations are a confederacy) reservations in western and upper New York State determined that the Mohawk are the most active producers: the greater part of them decorated baskets in natural colors of the wood (black ash) and sweet grass (figs. 41, 42), but some made splint or cornhusk utility pieces (fig. 43), such as a twilled corn washer/corn-hulling/corn-soup basket. Hominy cookery begins like this: After white shelled corn kernels have been boiled for up to an hour in water to which wood-ash had been added, the mass is dumped into a corn basket and held under running water. The lye in the wood ashes having partially decomposed the hulls, they loosen and can be flushed away through

FIGURE 44. Porcupine-curlicue decorated sewing basket by an Oneida (New York State) clan-mother, Delia Waterman, who learned from her grandmother; black ash, braided sweet-grass lifter: 1977. The use of one color (in this case, a rich, dark red) against the natural wood and the square-base-to-round-mouth construction both contribute to an earlier feeling. The weaver has incorporated both the pointed "porcupine" and the roll or ribbon variations of the curlicue overlay technique. O.H. 10″; Lid diam. 11½″.

holes in the bottom; the rougher texture of the twilled pattern of the sides is believed to aid in this removal. The corn is returned to the stove and cooked another twenty to forty-five minutes and again thoroughly rinsed. The boiling and rinsing process is repeated until the hulls have all fallen away and the water runs clear, at which point the corn is ready to be made into soup or bread, or fried.

The Mohawk community, named by them *Akwesasne*, is located along the Saint Lawrence River and designated on maps as the Saint Regis Indian Reservation. Although the tribespeople make no differentiation among themselves over it and one doesn't pass through a border station, part is within New York State, with the rest lying on the Canadian side.

Among the Senecas at the Cattaraugus Reserve, only a mother and daughter weave to sell; an "Indian Baskets for Sale" sign is posted on the former's front lawn. Figure 44 shows a new porcupine-curlicue covered basket, proof of current Oneida basketmaking.

WESTERN GREAT LAKES

A fair amount of Great Lakes basketwork goes on in Michigan and Wisconsin, and some in Minnesota. Although chiefly of the sweet-grass-decorated, black-ash-splint variety, persistence turned up the new coiled-grass trinket holder in figure 45. (I had wanted one without the commercial felt and beads that are commonly affixed to the covers of such containers.) Made by an old technique in the region, it is by a Michigan tribesman although Indian men seldom pursue basketmaking.

Wherever it grew, *Hierochloe odorata,* the true sweet grass' scientific name, was used as a personal perfume, burned as incense, and was an element in religious observances. It was also deemed to have the power to attract buyers to the baskets.

An old handled tray with birchbark around the sides (fig. 46) is probably Ottawa and may have been inspired by a form still prevalent in the southern Appalachians. The Ottawa tend to leave baskets undyed, whereas the Chippewa (Ojibwa) like a lot of color. New

FIGURE 45. Trinket holder of coiled sweet grass by a Michigan tribesman believed to be part Chippewa and part Ottawa, as most are in the Mackinaw City area where it was collected: 1975. The stitching is black cotton thread; the top has been made separately and connected with a thread hinge. Very old baskets, probably also Algonkian, were sewn with sinew. The center of the bottom is a piece of birchbark, which is pierced with the needle as the first coil is stitched to it all around, and each succeeding coil is sewn to the previous one. Small containers are the usual form this work takes; with a long history in the Great Lakes Region, it represents the only coiled basketry that persists there. Damp weather brings out its wonderful scent. H. 3"; Diam. 5¼".

FIGURE 46. Birchbark-decorated shallow, handled tray, black-ash splint (some a faded blue-green) with sweet grass, probably Ottawa (Michigan), as they used birchbark on other baskets in the early twentieth century. A similar shape but in rib-type construction is still being made by Southern Highlanders and seems once to have been made in New England and Pennsylvania. O.H. 7¾"; Diam. 9¼".

Wisconsin examples from both tribes are represented in figure 47. The Chippewa (who historically held unobtrusive sway over a vast territory) weave some in the north-central part of Minnesota, also.

The Winnebago at the Wisconsin Dells turn out a considerable number of sturdy baskets in a limited range of forms, and the

FIGURE 47. Ash baskets by the Ottawa and Chippewa of the Western Great Lakes, probably all commercial dyes, some sweet grass: all new except the old flattened, covered bowl (left foreground), which the author believes to be Chippewa. (Clockwise) Ottawa, Ottawa, tribe uncertain, Chippewa, Ottawa, Chippewa, and (right foreground) one from a basketmaking community of intermarried Ottawa and Chippewa (Peshabestown, Michigan). The Ottawa are more inclined to leave the natural color of the wood than are the Chippewa, who may dye all the splints for a basket, perhaps using a dark background (rear center). The diamond pattern is "never" used by contemporary Eastern Woodlands Indians but is common on old mats and bags. Tallest, said to be for berrying (firm berries, or they'd be crushed), is O.H. 18".

FIGURE 48. Miniatures from Western Great Lakes tribes, black ash, synthetic colors: 1976–1977. The three at far left are Winnebago (Wisconsin). Little handled baskets like the Ottawa (Michigan) at right rear are also made by the Winnebago. The "big" covered one is not quite 2½" high and incorporates natural splints, but most are dyed red, blue, yellow, or brown.

Menominee supply some to Door County (figs. 48, 49, the first of miniatures). The very limited output from the small Potawatomi Hannahville Indian Community on Michigan's Upper Peninsula near the Wisconsin line goes to local people or is promised in advance to dealers.

Basketry by Alaskan (Eskimo, Aleut, Haida, Tlingit) and Hawaiian Americans will be examined in chapter 6.

FIGURE 49. Winnebago and Menominee (Wisconsin) group, black ash, synthetic dyes: 1975, except shallow covered basket. It may be Winnebago and looks ten to twenty years old although remarkably similar in construction to the much older block-stamped bonnet basket in figure 38. (Rear, left to right) Menominee market basket and two-handled shopper. (Right end) Winnebago basket with movable handle intricately mounted in a manner also employed by the Cherokee of North Carolina. O.H. 15½"; Diam. 12½"–13" (slightly ovoid).

Memorandum
of Baskets &c.

Kept by the Basket Makers.

Also directions for weaving twilling
and proceeding with the work.

Recorded from 1855.

Commenced the Order of Baskets
Dec. 1, Finished April 30th 1856
Made 2230 for Sale, and 50 for fam-
ily and home use,
12 Hands viz. Anna Dodgson,
Julia Ann Scott, Maria ? Elizabeth
Cantrel, Ann M. Greaves, Ann E Scriven,
Eunice Cantrel, Lovina Belknap, Augusta
Stone, Adaline Cantrell, Julia Barker,
Cornelia French.

December 12th We are now in readiness
to commence our winter job of basketmaking. We have just finished 10 Doz.
which are to go immediately to N.Y.
Six Doz Spoon (3 Doz Covered) One Doz
Kitten Heads, Three Doz Cushion Bas.
Thus have filled our time and used
all the stuff we could get in Br Daniel's
absence. He has come home and
has so arranged matters that we have
a pretty good supply of nice stuff very
unexpectedly on hand.

For several years each hand has taken
a supply of baskets and seen to them; but
this year, we conclude to take each sort
and all work on them. So we now
commence the Spoon Baskets.
Seven hands are out of the Kitchen

FIGURE 50. Three pages excerpted from Shaker journal of basketweaving operations at New Lebanon (Mount Lebanon Community), New York, 1855–1874: "Memorandum of Baskets etc. Kept by the Basket Makers." These records show the Shop to have been "manned" by women as a winter occupation, with men probably supplying the dressed logs and perhaps preparing splint. Courtesy The Edward Deming Andrews Memorial Shaker Collection (no. SA-995), The Henry Francis du Pont Winterthur Museum, Winterthur, Delaware.

1869.

Commenced making Baskets Nov 24.
The names of those employed, are Julia
Ann S. Ann, Maria G. Augusta
S. Cornelia V. Fanny E. Emma E.
Anna B. Janette F. Ella H.
Mary K. Susanna M. Helena
W. a few weeks. A continual change
of experienced help for the young and
insufficient, is no great advantage to
this business. The winter past there
has been more constant failures in
the Shop occasioned by sickness than
I have known for 30 years. We finish
some time in August, as we have to
carry along our Spring & Summer work
besides, not having finished them as
is usual before this begins
The amount made is
2223

3

NEW FINDINGS FROM OLD BASKET-PRODUCING COMMUNITIES

THE SHAKERS

Less than two handfuls of "Shaking Quakers" reached New York in 1774, to suffer, among other trials, the suspicion of being British spies. But they numbered six thousand at nineteen locations in the East (New York and New England) and Midwest (Ohio, Indiana, and Kentucky) just prior to the Civil War. The celibate communards became renowned for their solid virtues and fine workmanship, but precipitously falling enrollment in the 1870s led to the eventual termination of the communities.

A journal of basketweaving operations at New Lebanon (Mount Lebanon), New York, from 1855 to 1874 is in The Edward Deming Andrews Memorial Shaker Collection at The Henry Francis du Pont Winterthur Museum, Winterthur, Delaware; three informative pages have been excerpted (fig. 50).

FIGURE 51. Selection from some three hundred Shaker baskets in the holdings at Sabbathday Lake, Maine, the sect's only ongoing residential community. Baskets were made, sporadically as needed, in the Mill Building. Most that remain at the community, many in use for laundry or herb or vegetable gathering, were made and remained there. Photograph courtesy The United Society of Shakers, Sabbathday Lake, Poland Spring, Maine; photograph by Steven D. Foster.

The sole community currently occupied by members of The United Society of Shakers is Sabbathday Lake near Poland Spring, Maine. Part of their museum's collection of about three hundred baskets, most of which have always been at the community, have been photographed for figure 51. A wash basket resembling others remaining there may be examined in figure 52.

The fine Mary Earle Gould Collection at Hancock Shaker Village, Hancock, Massachusetts, includes two interesting basketry imple-

FIGURE 52. Shaker wash basket/laundry carrier; ash splint, openwork bottom for drainage; came with Sabbathday Lake Community provenance and resembles several still there: c. 1860. O.H. 9″; Diam. 28″.

FIGURE 53. Funnel, black ash with hickory rim hoops. For transferring vinegar into kegs, it was first lined with cheesecloth. H. 16½″; Diam. 13″. A recent *National Geographic* article on Ladakh, India's most remote district, showed barley grain being funneled through a millstone by means of a basketry item quite like this. Photograph courtesy the Mary Earle Gould Collection, Hancock Shaker Village, Hancock, Massachusetts.

FIGURE 54. Ox muzzle, black ash. Intended to prevent the animal from succumbing to the distracting temptation to eat the crop. Whereas this muzzle was woven in hexagonal openwork, which was also used for cheese baskets, most muzzles were plain-plaited and fully enclosed. On the frontiers, strong, tractable oxen were the beasts of burden, but work horses were widely replacing them by the middle of the nineteenth century. H. 14½"; Diam. 14". Photograph courtesy the Mary Earle Gould Collection, Hancock Shaker Village, Hancock, Massachusetts.

ments: a funnel (fig. 53), and an ox muzzle (fig. 54), which was meant to discourage the creature from interrupting work to snatch a mouthful of tender crop shoots or tufts of grass along the way.

PENNSYLVANIA GERMANS

Early to arrive, there are still a lot of "Dutch" (Deutsch) in southeastern Pennsylvania, where Berks County has a town named Basket in 1884 for the trade initiated by a returning Civil War veteran, one Reuben Reifsnyder. This tidbit of history was gleaned from *Willow, Oak & Rye: Basket Traditions in Pennsylvania* by Jeannette Lasansky,

FIGURE 55. New, coiled rye-straw "beehive" baskets from Pennsylvania; by Carl Ned Foltz of Reinholds, who also teaches and is so busy that he has back orders more than two years old. (Rear) Two-handled open-top storage basket. (Foreground) Schnitz basket for keeping sliced dried apples; oval dough/bread-raising basket. (Center) Skeps or beehives, one in the process of manufacture; because he thought it would look interesting, Mr. Foltz was weaving this beehive with the grain left on the stems. The hollow skeps often had crossed sticks partway up the inside as a rude frame to support the honeycomb. Coiled-straw beehives have long been outlawed from use—presumably, they may have harbored or helped spread apiary diseases—but the name continues to be associated with baskets made with that technique. Finished hive, H. 15"; Diam. 18". Photograph courtesy Carl Ned Foltz, Reinholds, Pennsylvania; finished hive, Collection of Barbara L. Strawser.

published by the Union County Oral Traditions Projects in 1978. Along with detailed information about the usual types, there is coverage of the little-known rounded-oak basket, in which splints a quarter-of-an-inch square are whittled to a point at one end and pulled through holes in a custom die, resulting in round rods that simulate peeled willow withes.

Plate 9 shows old, and figure 55 new, coiled rye-straw or so-called beehive baskets. Actual straw hives went out when the wooden stacked-box sort came into general use by the midpoint of the nineteenth century, but baskets for storing food and clothing and those for dough-raising continued, probably because they afforded protection from mice (who refuse to chew them).

FIGURE 56. Lancaster County, Pennsylvania, market basket, peeled willow: duplicate commissioned from a slide issued by the Pennsylvania Farm Museum of Landis Valley, Lancaster, and made by Frank Selinsky of Hamilton, New York, 1977. These baskets came in both round and oval forms but are no longer being woven in Pennsylvania. O.H. 13¾"; Diam. 13½".

FIGURE 57. Lehigh County, Pennsylvania, potato basket, white oak: a very strong rib-type previously used by German settlers; made by John G. Long of Slatington: 1977. This 15″-diameter size holds one-half bushel, the capacity most commonly carried along the rows by potato pickers. As here, many were fitted with a set of outer splints called heels, runners, or drags (elsewhere called slides, cleats, skids, or shoes) for added protection during hard use; a buyer could order them inserted on a completed basket and paid extra. Mr. Long, whose great-uncle taught him, now puts his signature on his baskets at a buyer's request (see inside the handle), acting upon the advice of the Pennsylvania German Society.

A Lancaster County market basket (willow) and Lehigh County potato basket are shown in figures 56 and 57, the latter a rib-type oak-splint. Some of these were without handles but had openings under the rim for taking hold. Two strong men could carry firewood that way, or the basket could be more easily slipped under a hand-cranked corn sheller to catch the falling kernels. Yet another might be kept clean for laundry.

A seminar on baskets and makers in the state during the past three hundred years, a demonstration, coiled rye-straw workshops, and a special exhibition were part of the 1978 Institute of Pennsylvania Rural Life and Culture held at the Pennsylvania Farm Museum of Landis Valley near Lancaster.

THE AMANAS OF IOWA

One of a number of communal-living experiments (although the participants would never have called it that) on American soil was the Amana Colonies, seven villages established by eight hundred German-speakers who had tried New York State but moved onto purchased Iowa farm lands in 1855. Families lived together in their own quarters, but all work and its rewards were shared. The system was voted to an end in 1932.

FIGURE 58. Planting potatoes: spring 1910, West Amana, Iowa. Potatoes were part of every one of the three hearty, communally prepared meals each day. Baskets for field use were of unpeeled willow. Photograph courtesy Joan Liffring-Zug.

In figure 58, we observe a potato-planting crew, armed with the kind of willow baskets on which the Colonies' basketmaking concentrated. Plate 10 shows another unpeeled-willow utility basket, an apple-picking form distinctive in having a pair of small handles close to each other at the edge.

A sweet period photograph (fig. 59) has an old lady and a young girl with a more decorative household basket. Historic photographs also show coiled-straw shallow bowls filled with rising loaves, row upon row of them, lined up on tables and shelves at the Homestead bakery early in the century. An Amana man made them until the flour mill burned in 1923, after which rye ceased to be grown. The bakers repaired their old baskets with cord and needle, later resorted to bringing in rye straw to make new ones, and finally imported baskets.

There has been a struggling attempt in West Amana to revive the willow craft, but it is encountering difficulties in getting suitable osiers from a small cultivation.

LIVERPOOL, NEW YORK

Close to Syracuse, New York, once called Salt City for its brine wells, lies the town of Liverpool. Basketmaking began there when John Fischer, a recently arrived German immigrant who had found a job as a salt boiler, noticed the abundant stands of willows growing in the low-lying area and around 1850 began to weave baskets like those he'd made in his youth. So successful was his business that he brought over relatives and friends to join in, and burgeoning demand led a good many others to take up the craft.

Willow cultivation was introduced, and in the peak year of 1892 when production came close to 400,000, perhaps two thousand people were employed, some growing the willows, others preparing osiers (they were steamed in a closed box or shed and then the bark was stripped) or selling the finished baskets and furniture.

John Fischer's son George carried on. We have a photograph taken in his workroom around 1890 (fig. 60). The out-front display of a competitor, Seibel's, is figure 61. The basketmakers' homes ordi-

FIGURE 59. Amana women with a fine basket: believed to have been photographed c. 1910–1920. Perhaps the basket, obviously a prized possession, was featured in this charming pose because it was a gift for a special occasion. It is unlikely that either made the basket, for the craft was considered men's work in the Amana Colonies of Iowa. Baskets for the house were of peeled willow or, as here, made more attractive by incorporating both peeled and unpeeled willow. Similar baskets smaller in size were taken to knitting classes by the girls. Photograph courtesy Joan Liffring-Zug.

FIGURE 60. The George Fischer Basket Shop workroom, Liverpool, New York: c. 1890. The started basket bottoms were "pinned" to a special sloping bench, as seen here. Seated at left is the son of the German immigrant who founded the cottage industry in the community around 1850. Photograph courtesy Collection of Jasper T. Crawford, Liverpool, New York.

narily doubled as workshops and salesrooms for both peeled-willow furniture—chairs, tables, babies' and children's beds and buggies, lamps—and baskets. Some of the more enterprising establishments even published catalogues of their wares that could be specially ordered; Peter Duerr and Brothers offered well over two hundred items. Various shops turned out the same designs, as, for example, a hooded bassinet (fig. 62). A braided rim border is a distinguishing feature of the Liverpool baskets.

The cottage industry went into decline around World War I as the result of reduced demand and inroads made by competition from

FIGURE 61. Seibel's on Oswego Street, Liverpool, New York, view of sales display on front porch and lawn: c. 1900. Notice the colored bands incorporated into some of the baskets. Photograph courtesy Collection of Jasper T. Crawford, Liverpool, New York.

PLATE 1. Clam basket of splint, openwork bottom of multistrand heavy braided wire and wire ribs: nineteenth century The tops of the wire ribs are turned over to make hooks that catch onto a splint, which then was bound between two rim hoops. Other clam baskets are all splint. O.H. 13″; Rim 14¼″ x 13½″; 8″ sq. bottom. Collection of Mr. and Mrs. Donn P. Alspaugh.

PLATE 2. Fisherman's creel/trout basket with hand-carved wooden lid and original leather straps: probably last decade of the nineteenth century. The cover has incisions to mark the legal trout length and an oval opening so a fish could be slipped inside without lifting it. The deeply incurved back may have been custom-made to rest comfortably against its owner's paunch or midsection. H. 10″; L. 12¼″; Back to front 6¾″.

PLATE 3 (*Opposite*). Open-sided oval basket, found in New Hampshire, brushed with putty-colored paint: presumably late nineteenth century. One like it may be seen hanging up over a basketmaker's head in figure 67. Groups of rods in openwork fashion but with a scalloped rim are very common here and in Europe, the Orient, and even in North Africa and Central America. Willow was most commonly used in America, although honeysuckle vine came into some use after its introduction from Japan in the nineteenth century. H. 5″; L. 12½″; W. 11¾″. Photograph courtesy Frank and Barbara Pollack.

PLATE 4. Wood-bottomed baskets, oak splint: both probably late nineteenth century. (Left) A most unusual shape: an elongated diamond with rounded ends and curving sides. After the sides were woven, a specially made solid wood base was inserted to form the bottom, and then splint bands were placed around the circumferences of the sides at the rim and bottom edges and mounted on with many tiny nails so that the lower ends of the ribs (verticals) were held between the wooden band and the bottom board. Provenance unknown. O.H. 7″; L. 11¼″; W. 6″. Collection of Mr. and Mrs. Donn P. Alspaugh. (Right) Two boards, one outside and the other inside the basket, sandwich what must be an entire splint bottom. Collected in Massachusetts. O.H. 10½″; L. 19½″; W. 10¾″.

PLATE 5. Pomo (central California) feather-covered coiled basket; willow foundation with feathers from the meadowlark, woodpecker, mallard duck, quail (head plumes at the rim), and shell money; it still bears a label from Clear Lake, the location of one branch of the populous Pomo tribe: suggested date, late nineteenth or early twentieth century. Feathers were painstakingly worked onto the outside of the shallow bowl as the coiling proceeded. As many varieties of bright plumage were available, a group of the baskets presents a dazzling sight. These were bestowed as significant gifts, especially at marriage, cherished within the family, and customarily burned at funerals to honor the deceased. H. 2″; Diam. 12¼″. Photograph courtesy Collection of Ralph T. Coe.

PLATE 6. Hopi (northern Arizona) decorative baskets, coiled (Second Mesa) and wickerwork (Third Mesa) methods: mid-1970s. (Center foreground) Little plaque with eagle. (Clockwise) Deep bowl, antelope quartet on the march. H. 3¼″; Diam. 6″. Shalako kachina bust, a popular design, although the flat-bottomed shallow bowl is rare; by Louise Tenahhongva. Wickerwork plaque-trays: geometric, a checked star or sunburst; life themes, a butterfly suggesting movement (the medium's dynamic designs have been described as some of the most optically active in Indian art) and a nine-color masterwork by Regina Kooyahoema of a full-figure Ota (warrior-in-a-skirt) kachina, in a shield shape that best accommodates the motif. Coiled baskets are of shredded yucca or galleta-grass core bound with yucca; fresh leaves are green, sun-dried leaves are yellow, and the inner ones are white, and the two colors of black and a red-brown complete the palette. Wickerwork employs sumac or wild currant twigs as warp and/or rabbit brush for weft. Dyes may be either homemade plant, or mineral, or synthetic. (The rug is Navajo, of natural handspun wools in a Two Gray Hills pattern.)

PLATE 7. Koasati (Coushatta of Louisiana) elbow basket, river cane, bottom portion twilled and upper parts plain-plaited, chain motif in red and black: by Solomon Battise, collected new at the Coushatta Cultural Center in Elton, 1975. This is a gift basket, intended to contain small personal items and to be carried on the arm as a kind of purse (it hangs on the wall at other times). A similar basket is made nowadays of white oak by the Eastern Band of Choctaws. O.H. 16¾″; Greatest W. 15″; Ovoid openings 4″ x 3½″.

PLATE 9. Coiled rye-straw baskets from old German settlements, an assemblage from three collections: most of them probably from the last half of the nineteenth century. At right on top of the lovely Austrian *schrank* is an ambitious basket with wooden handles, an ingenious knob around which the cover was coiled, and a circular splint ring as a lashed-on foot. The flaring cone with flat strap across the rim was found in Berks County, Pennsylvania. Its purpose is a mystery, although it is speculated that it held nuts or fruit drying by the fireplace before their transfer to a storage basket. The body of the 22″-long covered oblong in foreground, quite likely a food carrier, was made in two pieces, with the base bound onto a finished body, and came out of northern Ohio. Baskets with carrying handles are uncommon in construction, because they lack the strength to transport heavy loads, nor would the attachment of the handle be likely to stand up. Photograph courtesy Mr. and Mrs. Lee N. Hames and Mrs. Mildred Heck.

PLATE 8. Choctaw (Mississippi) three-tiered pocket knife-and-fork basket (wall-hung), swamp cane, synthetic dyes: by Jeffie Solomon of the Conehatta Community, collected new through the Choctaw Craft Association at Philadelphia, 1975. This form descends from an earlier type with squared-off pockets that has been made by Eastern Woodlands tribes both for their own use and for sale (fig. 38). O.H. 20½"; Bottom pocket 11" across and 6½" front to back.

PLATE 10. Amana Colonies of Iowa apple-picking basket, unpeeled willow: late nineteenth century. The Amana Heritage Society says a good-sized metal hook would have been attached to one of the handles and the basket suspended from a branch of the apple tree. A smaller, peeled version of the form was a strawberry basket, and its pair of handles, close together on the rim, served as loops to slip a belt through or otherwise hang it at one's waist. O.H. 14"; Diam. 14½".

PLATE 11 *(Above, left)*. Peeled-osier (willow-twig) flower holder, after one from the Liverpool, New York, cottage industry, c. 1940: copy made by Frank Selinsky of Hamilton, New York, 1977. (The original is owned by Richard G. Case of Syracuse, New York.) Mr. Selinsky rubber-stamps his name and address on the outside of the bottom of each basket he makes. This replica is O.H. 24¼″; L. 17½″; W. 13½″.

PLATE 12 *(Opposite)*. Nantucket (Massachusetts) Lightship Baskets, old and new, rattan with wooden bottom boards. (Left) An early traditional open basket, with base shaped by a spokeshave or similar hand instrument rather than having been turned on a lathe. An outline of its lost gummed label remains. H. (without handle) 5½″; L. 12¾″; W. 10¾″. (Right) Covered handbag with ivory fittings and whale-tooth carving on lid: made to order in 1966 by Stephen S. Gibbs, who burned "S. GIBBS" and the words "MAKER" and "NANTUCKET, MASS." on the bottom. O.H. 11¼″; L. 9½″; W. 6¾″. Both antique and contemporary Lightship Baskets cost hundreds of dollars, and customers willingly wait months for custom-made baskets from present-day artisans.

PLATE 13 *(Left)*. Green unpeeled-willow fruit baskets like those the Italian-born maker had, as a child, watched his uncle weave; they were made to fill a request by Dominick Masi of Rome, New York: 1977. Although these baskets turn brown as the switches dry, they are initially as bright as a thickly painted pea-soup yellow-green. Largest, O.H. 16½"; Diam. 16"–18".

PLATE 14. Coiled baskets, most collected from their various Afro-American sewers at Mount Pleasant, Charleston County, South Carolina: 1977. (Front) *Fanna* (fanner) basket; the old form was used to winnow rice. A deeper version was called a vegetable basket and, balanced on the head, transported produce. Diam. 17″. (Middle, left to right) Pedestal flower or fruit basket. "Fancy" basket, a lovely deep platter exhibiting an ornamental technique in which coils are bound away from the body to form an openwork border. (Top, left to right) "Missionary" basket reputedly for carrying the Bible to church but now often described by vendors as a handbag. In-and-out basket, a distinctive line associated with the modern-period Sea Islands craft, Oval shopping basket with French knots of brown pine needles; the maker herself takes such a basket marketing. The coil foundations are bundles of a tall wild grass, and the bindings are strips of palmetto fronds with dry pine needles or a gold-colored rush worked in to achieve patterning.

PLATE 15 *(Below)*. Half-basket, intended to be hung with the flat side against a wall, a form still being turned out in the mountains of the South by both whites and the Cherokee of North Carolina, white-oak splint: this one has a little age on it. One researcher (Stephenson, see Selected Bibliography) found them referred to as key baskets and learned that they were related to those in which mistresses of plantations had kept their keys to the household's storerooms. O.H. 6¼″; L. 10¼″; W. 4¼″.

PLATE 16. Rib-type oak-splint baskets from a third-generation basketmaking couple in the Missouri Ozarks, Leslie and Gussie Jones of Branson: 1974. A good many oak-splint baskets are woven in the Arkansas Ozarks, but they're not of this more difficult construction. Largest, O.H. 13¼″; L. 17½″; W. 13″.

PLATE 17. Alaskan Eskimo coiled basket with snugly fitting knobbed lid (the knob is hollow), dried grasses; purchased new through The Alaska Native Arts & Crafts Cooperative Association, Inc.: 1974. Either geometric or representational motifs are typically widely spaced and placed in rows, with the colored grass strands dyed with natural or commercial dyes. I have also noticed this stylized flower on a finely woven twined Aleutian basket. O.H. 9½″.

PLATE 18. Deep market basket with brass-studded and lapped rim, a woodworking technique, black ash: end of the nineteenth century. Details strongly suggest Indian manufacture: its shape, the use of black ash cut into thin, narrow splints, and the turning over and tucking inside of the tops of alternate ribs. Market or shopping baskets typically served double duty as gathering baskets in the backyard vegetable patch, and the openwork bottom of this one—where soil remains in the grooves—was intended to facilitate the rinsing off of the dirt. This is the only basket I've seen that incorporates big-headed upholsterer's nails; they're not simply ornamental but fix the rim to the splints, and the handle attachment is reinforced with a pair of long iron nails at each end. O.H. 14¾″; Squared bottom 12½″ x 5¼″.

PLATE 19. Incised wide-splint basket found in Maine; smooth and shiny rim and binding may be maple: possibly 1870s. The motif, a semicircle of radiating lines resembling a setting (or is it rising?) sun, has been burned in. The basket looks Scandinavian, in that the plaiting is handled rather as if it were birchbark. Even though the manner of binding on the rim is not at all Indian and Indians would have applied the design by "potato"-stamping rather than by hot-branding (and never to the handle), this example came identified as "Maine Indian"; but it does impart an Indian "feeling" that I cannot quite put my finger on. The only two I've seen similar in construction, although without incisions, lacked provenance, so its origin remains a mystery. O.H. 11″; Diam. 12″.

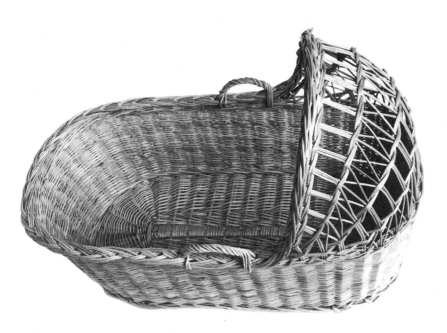

FIGURE 62. Bassinet/baby bed or carrier, peeled willow, after No. 166 in Peter Duerr & Bros. (established 1884) catalogue, Liverpool, New York: copy made to order by Frank Selinsky of Hamilton, New York, 1977. H. 23″; L. 34½″; W. 18¼″. A variant of this model had a single high handle crossing over, rather than opposing handles for lifting. A bassinet on legs was also offered; one appears in figure 61 of the Seibel's shop outdoor display about 1900, as well as in a c. 1960 photograph of one of the last basketmakers with his "willow-ware."

imports and factory-made goods. None of the shops remained beyond the early 1960s. One man still weaves in the Liverpool tradition. He is Frank Selinsky of Hamilton, New York, whose family lived next door to a basketmaker who had taught his father. Little Frank was finishing his first piece, a small hamper, by the age of nine. Mr. Selinsky earlier had a roadside shop at Bouckville. He executed three baskets shown in this book, among them the flower basket in plate 11. In an interview,[8] he recalled an occasion when he filled an order for 144 different kinds of flower baskets for Valentine Brothers, florists, and used the $75 proceeds to buy himself an iceboat.

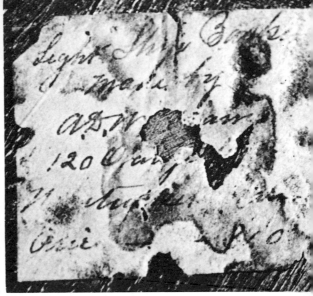

FIGURE 64. Close-ups of original paper labels pasted on old Nantucket Lightship Baskets by their makers, one printed and the other handwritten. Davis Hall, a crew member on the lightship anchored off Nantucket Island, glued his label to the outside bottom of the largest basket in the six-piece nest shown in the preceding photograph. A. D. Williams lived and worked there during the early and middle 1920s; a surprising number of his labels have survived. More recently, Nantucket basketmakers have been carving or burning their identification into the outside of the bottom board or, less common, fastening on a little plaque. Photograph by Richard Merrill, Saugus, Massachusetts.

FIGURE 63. Nest of six Nantucket Lightship Baskets, rattan and turned-wood bottoms: made by Davis Hall, whose name appears on the pay list for late 1881 and who served on the South Shoals Lightship under Captain Andrew Sandsbury to 1891. Nesting sets are rarely found, most having been split up along the way; the individual baskets fetch hundreds of dollars and nests several thousand. This is a particularly fine set, not only for careful workmanship, which is usual, but in proportions, graduation of sizes, and especially the graceful handles. Sizes from O.H. 14″ with Diam. 11¾″ to O.H. 7¾″ and Diam. 5″¾. Photograph by Richard Merrill, Saugus, Massachusetts.

NANTUCKET ISLAND, MASSACHUSETTS

Prices for antique Nantucket Lightship Baskets seem to be "holding up," as an expert-collector wryly remarked in recounting the story of a recent experience at an auction, where he, fighting for "a beauty with rosewood bottom . . . went to $525, and lost it to the next bid." Although some dealers had anticipated that prices had topped and would come down, he'd been seeing only damaged ones at significantly lower prices. Brand-new ones are running ever higher, too.

A magnificent six-basket nest bearing Davis Hall's paper label appears in figure 63. Figure 64 has his label and that of A. D. Williams. Two oval Lightship Baskets sit side by side in plate 12, one a covered handbag version of a type that has been made for about thirty years with carved ivory or whale-tooth top ornament and fittings.

There are perhaps ten or twelve active Lightship Basket weavers on Nantucket. An artisan working full time might be able to finish seventy baskets in a year; turned-wood bottom boards and the ivory carvings are obtained from local sources, with the weavers, as always, of imported rattan.

THE SOLITARY
BASKETMAKER

Dudley H. Frasure of Sherburne, New York, was the ultimate solitary basketmaker. By choice, he lived alone in a log cabin on Hunt's Mountain for five years, during which time he taught himself to make a couple of dozen different kinds of ash-splint baskets. After his return to the family farmstead in the Chenango Valley, he specialized in the Adirondack pack basket (fig. 65), of which he has by now finished and sold over two thousand.

In 1945 he and a friend had needed something in which to carry their supplies. A shop owner suggested making their own pack baskets, providing a sketchy description of the Indian technique for pounding an ash log so that the annual growth rings separate and the wood comes away in lengthwise strips that can be processed into splints. They finally managed it, and the friend went his way. Mr. Frasure stayed with it.

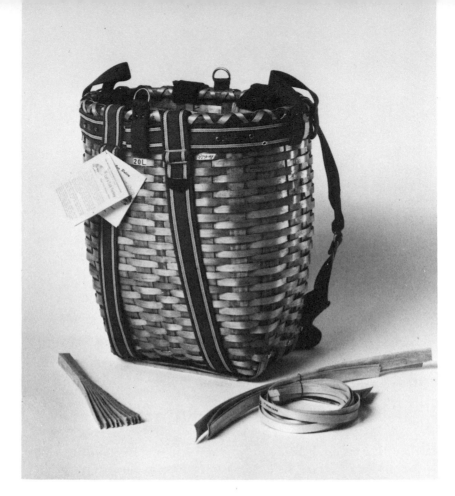

FIGURE 65. Adirondack (New York State) pack/backpack basket, white ash, shellacked yellow, complete with special emerald-and-gold-striped harness, by Dudley H. Frasure of Sherburne, New York: 1978. Mr. Frasure bills his design as a comfortable carryall for hunting, hiking, camping, trapping, fishing, and winter sports. This is his best-selling size, a #20 Large (20″ high) with ⅝-bushel capacity, suitable for a man five feet ten inches tall and weighing approximately 150 to 170 pounds. Mr. Frasure is a justly proud craftsman and affixes metal identification plates; the sticker gives the retail price of $79.95. He thoughtfully encloses a few splints against the possibility of future damage (a tag explains how to insert them). Mr. Frasure pounds white-ash logs for splint, a harder job than with black ash; the billet demonstrates how the wood layers separate along growth rings after pounding.

He still works alone and told a reporter for the *Chenango Union* (October 7, 1975): "This is a one-man factory. I couldn't teach this to anyone else. They would have to live with me to learn. There's part of me in every one of these baskets."

Mr. Frasure enjoyed his half-decade opportunity to "live deliberately" in the woods, as Thoreau advised, but came out in 1950 because he was urgently needed at home (a farm that has been in his family since 1877) and because his growing pack basket and commercial Christmas wreath businesses called for a location that would be more convenient for delivery. Although visitors did drop by from time to time, there was no mail or other service to the top of his mountain. Mr. Frasure had been inundated with pack basket orders following his appearance in demonstrations at the New York State Fair, September 5–10, 1949, and gained further prestige when Abercrombie & Fitch in New York City featured his pack baskets in their store and catalogues of quality sporting goods. But he discontinued the association when the baskets' reputation brought him more orders than he could fill closer by; current production is limited to about seventy-five a year, ranging in size from 16 inches and one-third-bushel capacity to 24 inches and one-and-a-half bushel. Mr. Frasure takes much satis-

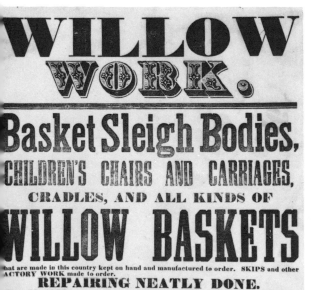

FIGURE 66. Broadside for "WILLOW WORK" by Wm. Washington of West Chester, Pennsylvania: 1858. Some other basket shops also sold wooden ware and/or carried imported baskets such as French and German "Fancy Baskets." Note that Mr. Washington's circular proclaims "made in this country" and emphasizes with large type: "REPAIRING NEATLY DONE." Courtesy the Joseph Downs Manuscript Collection (no. 76 X 66), The Henry Francis du Pont Winterthur Museum, Winterthur, Delaware.

FIGURE 67. Willow-basket artisan amid the clutter of his work and sales area: taken from a stereopticon card (the craze began here in the 1850s and raged in the 1890s). The craftsman has assembled a striking variety of baskets for the photograph. Hanging above and slightly to his right is an oval open-sided basket like that in plate 3. Photograph courtesy America Hurrah Antiques, New York City.

FIGURE 68. Ash-splint baskets in two weaves by a New England crafts-woman, Mary L. Tilley of Ashfield, Massachusetts: 1977. The weaver, who took up the craft with great enthusiasm in recent years, was a student of Wayne Rundell, whose work is shown in figure 12, and has taught, too. It was a surprise to find someone doing hexagonal openwork, which is eco-nomical of material but not of time. Mrs. Tilley was fascinated with the idea of carving handles into shapes after seeing one on an old basket in my previous book. She has become an innovator and even filled a request for a handle with a clasped-hands motif, which was wanted by a scrimshaw fancier who had admired the design in scrimshanders' ivory pieces. The square-bottomed knitting basket on pointed "feet" (upper right) is 7¼" high and almost 10" in diameter. Note the intricate handling of the ends of the movable bail on the egg basket at bottom.

faction in his basketmaking but must attend to income-augmenting sideline activities in order to support himself with a few personal comforts in his preferred modest rural life-style.

While there is a great deal of interest on the part of the public in buying baskets, most artisans find it a problem to set prices that match the work involved, especially since many have little choice about where they live. For the most isolated, getting the baskets to where they can be sold frequently presents a problem.

Back when everyone needed baskets as a matter of course, customers were reached by going the rounds peddling or by luring them into the shop with printed advertising pieces like "Wm. Washington's" 1858 broadside (fig. 66). An anonymous willow-basket maker appears in figure 67, originally a stereopticon card; he's whipped up quite a display of his versatility and industry.

Numerous basketweavers represented in this book work out of their homes in rural or small-town locations far removed from others practicing the craft, or at least are not part of a basketmaking community. Dominick Masi of Rome, New York, who learned willow-work from an uncle in his native Italy long ago, is one (pl. 13). So is Mary L. Tilley of Ashfield, Massachusetts, although she has done some teaching and shows at craft fairs; four of her baskets have been photographed for figure 68, including two in hexagonal openwork.

Distance from a market is especially prevalent in much of the southern Appalachians and is generally an obstacle to anyone who is not part of a community of such artisans. The support and sharing of having craft fellows nearby, the opportunity to learn early on, and to advance one's skills under expert tutelage, all can be of inestimable benefit. The nitty-gritty advantages of residence in a group whose reputation for a special kind of product attracts people to the vicinity and/or proximity to a resort area are definite pluses.

SOUTHERN BASKETS

A special kind of work is the cotton-stitched plaiting of split young palmetto leaves, as practiced in southwestern Louisiana by Cajun (French Acadians who migrated from Nova Scotia around 1750, when the British took over) or Houma craftswomen, types shown in figure 69.

The rest of Southern basketmaking falls into three distinct classifications, of which the first, tribal work—chiefly by the Cherokee of North Carolina, Seminole and Miccosukee of Florida, Choctaw (Mississippi), Koasati (Coushatta of Louisiana), and the Alabama-Coushatta of eastern Texas—has been covered in chapter 2.

MOUNT PLEASANT, SOUTH CAROLINA, AFRO-AMERICAN COILING

Revisiting Charleston in the spring of 1977, I observed the coastal "Low Country's" substantial Gullah-speaking (a Creole language that

FIGURE 69. Louisiana palmetto baskets, plaited and stitched with white cotton thread: mid-1970s. Leaves taken from the heart of the plant just before they emerge are laboriously cured over several days, then split. (Right) The lady who sold me this bowl said she remembered when Cajun (French Acadian) ladies made themselves big-brimmed hats by sewing plaited strips together in this way. H. 6½"; Diam. 9½". (Left) "Crisscross" handbag by a Houma weaver; others plait table mats. L. 11¾"; W. 9"; D. 10".

incorporates many African words) community vigorously pursuing their basketry. Among changes since my 1974 research trip was the presence of artisans selling in the reopened Old City or Public Market. It was Saturday, and some of them concentrate on being there then because that's the busiest day. Their wares were spread on the floor

FIGURE 70. Basket stand on U.S. Highway 17 north of Mount Pleasant near Charleston, South Carolina: 1978. This is Ethel Mae Snipe's stand, one of sixty-some in the immediate area that are operated by families making and selling the coiled "Low Country" or Sea Islands baskets. The transplanted craft had its origins in Africa, and the technique has been in continuous use here since the eighteenth century. Materials and designs have undergone substantial changes. Photograph by Greg Day.

(roofed buildings) or sidewalk, with most offering their own baskets and demonstrating how they are made by plying a homemade awl fashioned from the handle of a metal teaspoon. (In basket sewing, the implement pierces an opening into the preceding coil so a wefting strip can be pushed and pulled through.) Buying was brisk, the bulk of it by residents rather than tourists, judging from the accents and attire.

A couple of vendors frequented the "Four Corners of Law," the downtown intersection of Meeting and Broad streets (site of the former state legislature, now the county courthouse; city hall; post office; and Saint Michael's Church, once the legal, that is, official church).

Driving north along U.S. Highway 17 beyond Mount Pleasant, close to half of the sixty-odd roadside basket stands on the almost four-mile stretch were open for business (see one in fig. 70). Specific vendors would be difficult to locate, because some move to other stands or may not be out regularly, depending upon how much they have to sell and the demands upon their time. I saw more younger weavers than I had three years earlier, a sign of the occupation's growing economic viability; this was confirmed by what appeared to be close to a fifty percent increase in prices. A good-sized basket for which I might have paid $18 in 1974 now cost $25—and seemed, mysteriously, to have managed to shrink a bit in size, to boot.

This is the most vital basketmaking community in the United States today, in the sense of involvement of a large population and the continual evolution of designs. There may be fifteen hundred people participating—gathering materials, often from far away, sewing, selling.

Figures 71 and 72 and plate 14 picture baskets collected in 1977. Figure 71 includes, for comparison, a recent African basket made by the Ovambo people, who live in present-day Angola and Namibia (previously South-West Africa, a protectorate administered by South Africa). Plate 14 has a rice fanner, or *fanna* basket. Rice cultivation was an African introduction, as was the making of shallow, round coiled trays for winnowing the grain after it had been pounded to break open the husk. The basket is shaken so that its contents are

FIGURE 71. Mount Pleasant, South Carolina, coiled-grass baskets shown with a recent African basket: mid-1970s. (Foreground) Ovambo basket, from a tribe living in a territory that covers part of both Namibia (formerly South-West Africa) and Angola. During the late eighteenth century slaves brought into South Carolina came from the Congo-Angola and Senegambia regions. Twentieth-century baskets from the last-named also resemble Carolinian baskets. Although core material shows between the stitches on the bottom of the Ovambo piece, it is completely hidden on the sides and top by an overlay strip. The dry pine needles in the American baskets would not be available in much of Africa; however, the incorporation of dark brown fibers for decorative effect appears, too. (Left) O.H. 11¾".

tossed up into the air, and the wind blows away the light husks—the chaff.

In 1978/79, The Cleveland Museum of Art circulated the exhibition "The Afro-American Tradition in Decorative Arts," which incorporated a number of contemporary Afro-American baskets along

with older examples. The catalogue (by John Michael Vlach, see Selected Bibliography) points out that coiled rice fanners are present throughout Africa and quite common in Angola, from which area came (as slaves) the forebears of many Carolinians. From the technology employed by men who made this basic two-foot-diameter agricultural tool, the American materials for which consisted of bundles of bulrush bound with narrow palmetto-butt splints or white oak, women moved on to develop domestic-use designs and to work with local wild grasses (*Sporobolus gracilis* and related species) and palmetto leaf, sometimes adding dry brown pine needles for visual effect.

Mount Pleasant basket stands began to spring up when the paving of the coastal highway between Charleston and Georgetown during the 1920s brought through increased traffic. Sometimes referred to as Sea Islands (a chain along the coasts of South Carolina, Georgia, and northern Florida) basketry, it is practiced today all but exclusively near Mount Pleasant and nowhere else commercially.

Face of an Island (New York: Grossman Publishers, 1971) by Edith M. Dabbs features Leigh Richmond Miner's early 1900s photographs taken on Saint Helena Island (near Beaufort, South Carolina); among them is one of Alfred Graham, the first teacher of basketry at Penn School, a man who had brought the skill with him from Africa as a youth. One of her captions calls a boy's nickname a "basket name," presumably a reference to his baby bed, although I had not previously heard this usage. Several of the photographs show baskets.

Another informative reading on the subject is Gerald L. Davis's recent essay, "Afro-American Coil Basketry in Charleston County, South Carolina,"[9] which contains verbatim interviews with basketmakers, some providing conflicting historical detail.

FIGURE 72. Mount Pleasant, South Carolina, hanging planters; two craftswomen view a popular form: 1977. (Bottom) Albertha Lewis adds an important shield surround; O.H. 16½"; W. 14". (Top) Mary Jane Manigault lets the funnel-shape carry the piece. Designs are constantly evolving among the numerous Afro-American basketmakers in the locale, and individualization is a matter of pride.

I find it fascinating to collect in the area for the sheer breadth of choice, the opportunity for direct communication, and because, although the African technique doesn't vary, individual forms are ever changing. Keen attention among the basketsewers to each other's work is, in effect, a sort of informal competition wherein one might jealously guard a design innovation from another's prying eyes. Some of the most skillful and experienced will accept custom orders for

FIGURE 73. White-oak utility baskets from the Deep South: 1975. Plain and sturdy, with no time wasted on achieving perfect symmetry or on unnecessary smoothing of the rough splints—this kind of finishing might result in some thinning and, therefore, weakening of the weavers. (Right) Hanging mail basket, by Edward Harris; bought in a large hardware store in Opelousas, Louisiana, where a quantity of handwoven utility baskets were offered for sale. O.H. 15¾"; L. 7"; W. 5¼". (Left) A basket for gathering potatoes and such from the home garden, by Mississippian Leon Clark. O.H. 14¾"; Diam. 8½".

FIGURE 74. "Cotton picking," splint baskets in the fields: a photograph taken by George François Mugnier between 1880 and 1910 and published in a book on his work, *New Orleans and Bayou Country* (Barre, Mass.: Barre Publishers, 1972), edited by Lester Burbank Bridaham. The picked cotton was put into sacks dragged along the ground, then emptied into baskets left at the ends of the rows, and these were taken to a wagon or elsewhere. Cotton baskets—some are still being made for picking from small private patches in the Deep South—are of white oak or ash and usually have openings under the rim as handholds. Photograph courtesy Barre Publishers.

variations on a line or even execute a client's entirely original idea.

Afro-Carolinian baskets are surfacing more often in stores. I've encountered them in Georgia and New York City, and one collector told me that, having purchased my earlier book in a small town in Indiana and having read it while waiting for lunch, she just happened to stroll past a shopwindow full of Mount Pleasant baskets.

WHITE-OAK SPLINT FOR UTILITY

Although the Mount Pleasant Afro-American coiled work and the Indian basketmaking may be considered more noteworthy, in former times by far the greatest bulk of baskets made in the South were plain white-oak splint meant for utilitarian purposes. Some can be bought today (two appear in fig. 73). Notice the rough splints; little time has been spent in finishing, but they are meant to last. One craftsman was quite honest, albeit short on tact, when he assured a young customer at a fair that one of his baskets would probably outlast *her*. (She seemed somewhat jarred by the prospect.) In an age accepting of speedy obsolescence, basketmakers in the Deep South are still turning out baskets built to survive decades of daily use.

And even today, cotton baskets like those shown in the field in figure 74 hold cotton that has been raised in small family patches and picked by hand. (Of course, the percentage of our annual crop that ever enters a hand-woven cotton basket is slight.) A Georgia man, Sam Davis of Willacoochee, who demonstrates at the Georgia Agrirama at Tifton, has woven cotton baskets that could hold three hundred pounds of seed cotton. Perhaps one reason Southerners cling to handmade baskets is they can get them; I saw a large pile of fresh oak-splint baskets in the biggest hardware store in Opelousas, Louisiana.

Whereas in the Delta and the coastal plains most basketmakers seem to be black men, the weavers of Appalachia are both white men and women. The Southern Highlands were settled by people of mainly Anglo-Saxon stock who brought rib-type construction with them from Europe (see two egg baskets in fig. 75). Wall baskets like that in plate 15 sell well. An older example of a wood basket (fig. 76) exhibits walnut-stained splints.

Photographed in plate 16 is a group of sturdy rib-types from a third-generation basketmaking couple in Missouri. The Ozarks were

FIGURE 75. Egg baskets from the Southern Appalachian Mountains, white oak. (Right) Collected new in the Great Smokies in 1962. O.H. 9¾"; Rim 8¾" x 7½". (Left) Finely woven basket by Mary Prater, who lives near Nashville, Tennessee, and learned from an older sister; her sister-in-law is also a basketmaker. This basket, with closely woven narrow splints and covered handle, retailed in the North for $50 in 1977, as compared with another of the same size but with wider splints and uncovered splint handle that sold for $28. O.H. 9"; Rim diam. 8½".

homesteaded by Southern Highlanders, who must have been happy with the similar topography. Their basketry had to a great extent died out in Arkansas before its revival in the early 1960s; a quantity of oak-splint baskets with twilled bottoms are being made and sold in Arkansas, although the rib-types are not being made there.

FIGURE 76. Appalachian wood/firewood/log/chip/ kindling carrier and storage basket, now often used for magazines; brown-dyed bands: probably dates from early in this century. O.H. 11⅝"; L. 21"; W. 12½". Photograph by Helga Photo Studio, New York.

FROM BEYOND OUR
CONTERMINOUS BORDERS

HAWAII

Formerly known as the Sandwich Islands, the north Pacific group comprising the Hawaiian Islands proudly became the fiftieth state, Hawaii, on August 21, 1959.

Basketmaking hardly exists today, but the genus pandanus was in the past the leading tree for a wide range of mat and basket applications that demanded flexibility with durability. The coco palm leaves were plaited into paneling that was favored for constructing the sides and roof of temporary verandas, or *lanai,* and grasses, ferns, aerial roots, and sennit from the outer covering of the coconut also served in basketry. More prized than most baskets were choice *makaloa,* mats of sedge grass; the finest were worn as partial body coverings. Some became famous, and one was even named and handed down as having

FIGURE 77. Hawaiian checker-work-plaited bag of *hala* (pandanus) leaves: 1976. In a day spent scurrying about Honolulu, on the telephone and on foot, in search of living basketry, this was the only piece I could garner. It is merely a present-day application of a mat-making technique once common in the Pacific Islands, which I was able to get at the shop in the Bernice P. Bishop Museum. Of course, there are very simple baskets being woven of split coconut-palm fronds, made like the hats that tourists buy, but I did not find them offered for sale. They seemed to materialize only as packages arriving with gift fruit, and I failed to enlist a hotel staffer to scout up a guest's discard. O.H. 16″; L. 14½″; W. 6″.

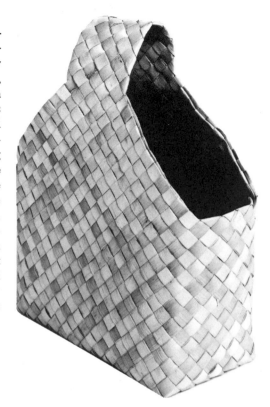

been part of a king's raiment on the occasion of his meeting his future wife.

Images of gods, principally the fierce war-god Kukailimoku, were constructed of wickerwork and covered with a net to which were attached red, yellow, and black feathers. More ordinary items were hats and sandals, fans (against heat and flies), combs, satchels, pillows (small cubical ones answered as balls in games), wrestling mats, and eating or sleeping mats, as well as boat sails, spears and clubs, shields, and a unique high helmet that gave superb protection from blows.

A thorough source of information is William T. Brigham's well-illustrated "Mat and Basket Weaving of the Ancient (Old) Hawaiians," published in 1906 in the *Memoirs of the Bernice Pauahi Bishop Museum.* The only substantial collection of Hawaiian basketry of which I am aware belongs to that museum in Honolulu. Their shop was the only place I could buy an indigenous basket in 1976, a bag checkerwork-plaited of pandanus leaves (fig. 77), its bottom a squared mat continued vertically. It's perfect evidence of Brigham's statement that ". . . there is no convenient partition between basket and mat; a basket is a folded-up mat, or a mat is a basket opened out, especially in the forms most common in the Pacific."

FIGURE 78. Valuable Attu (Aleut) twined-grass baskets: of museum quality, these antiques were valued in the mid-1970s at $2,100 and $1,800. The collecting, curing, and preparation of the beach rye grass is a lengthy procedure, but its painstaking weaving has created some of the finest baskets known. Aboriginal women wove shrouds and were encouraged by Russians who moved in in the mid-eighteenth century to try baskets; their influence also led to incorporation of silk and cotton thread in motifs. H. 4"–5". Photograph courtesy The Alaska Native Arts & Crafts Cooperative Association, Inc., Anchorage, Alaska.

ALASKA

Russian names still linger in the territory that joined the Union as its forty-ninth sovereign state on January 3, 1959.

The prevalent southwest coastal Eskimo basket is grass-coiled in the form of a jar with a tight, knobbed cover and wide-spaced rows of representational or geometric designs (pl. 17). Aleut pieces are often referred to as *Attu baskets,* for the outermost island of the Aleutian chain, source of the famous rye-grass twined basketry (see two museum-quality examples in fig. 78). There has been a resurgence of interest in this work, and the baskets are being featured in art

FIGURE 79. Tlingit and Haida (southeastern Alaska) twined spruce-root containers, false embroidery motifs in natural dyes obtained from berries and minerals: mid-1970s. (Left) Made by Selina Peratrovich of Ketchikan, priced at $238. H. 5¼"; Diam. 5½". The others are by Annie Lawrence of Hoonah, $210 and $225. Representational designs are also employed. It is traditional for the knobs to contain the gizzard stones of a bird so that they emit a rattling sound, but now shot is replacing them. Photograph courtesy The Alaska Native Arts & Crafts Cooperative Association, Inc., Anchorage, Alaska.

FIGURE 80. Puerto Rican two-handled deep bowl of split aerial roots of *bejuco de cupey*, a native vine: 1975. O.H. 7½"; Diam. 12".

exhibitions in the "Great Land," as its Eskimo people were first to call it.

The Panhandle of southeastern Alaska holds two resident Northwest Coast–culture Indian tribes, the Haida and the Tlingit, who are producing twined spruce-root containers (fig. 79). In the past, the Haida were most noted for large, distinctive twined hats onto which clan designs were painted. The Tlingit had special watertight cups from which they drank saltwater during a purification rite; their mythology is filled with legends of baskets of magical origin.

The source for the baskets shown in these photographs was The Alaska Native Arts & Crafts Cooperative Association, a marketing organization of Eskimo and Indian craftsmen that is headquartered in Anchorage and has shops there and in Juneau.

COMMONWEALTH OF PUERTO RICO

On July 25, 1952, the Caribbean island of Puerto Rico became a

Commonwealth voluntarily associated with the United States under a contract approved by Congress and a vote by Puerto Ricans.

A few years ago, a relative toured several San Juan shops in search of the baskets of Puerto Rico. Although he saw a good many new baskets for sale, figure 80 shows the only one that could then be positively identified by sellers as local in manufacture.

Being unable to make a research trip in person, I began correspondence with a member of the Department of Anthropology at the University of Puerto Rico, who became my principal informant. There are some twenty or more active basketmakers dispersed at scattered locations. There is coiling of *palma de cogollo*, also called *palma de sombrero*; splintwork with *bejuco de paloma*; and wicker with *bejuco de cupey*, as well as the manufacture of *jipijapa* hats of *palma de cogollo* fiber.

An old form that is made in different sizes is a deep splint for harvesting coffee beans on plantations. It is shown at the rear in figure

81, which includes a large two-handled coffee basket and egg and bread baskets, some of them coiled. Other baskets have been employed for vending farm produce, drying meat, storing linens, horse pack baskets (as a pair, one hanging at each side), and as baby beds. The lion's share of production goes for utilitarian purposes. There is some street peddling, but most of the distribution is through shops.

A good selection of Commonwealth baskets is carried at the Centro de Artes Populares (Folk Arts Center) shop, which is sponsored by the Institute of Puerto Rican Culture and housed at the Dominican Convent in Old San Juan. Here, one can also find permanent and temporary exhibits and obtain the names and addresses of basketmakers who welcome visitors to their workshops. A 1978 Weaving Festival at Isabela, held under that organization's auspices, included *canastas* (baskets) and demonstrations of basketry, and I am told that a film about the craft is being prepared.

FIGURE 81. A gathering of the varied baskets of the Commonwealth of Puerto Rico: 1978. (Left) Coiled of *palma de cogollo* fiber by Eufemio Lopez of Aguadilla; the 12"-diameter round one resembles some Haitian work. (Clockwise) Two kinds of coffee harvesting baskets. The smaller, which is held by pickers, is of *bejuco de paloma* by Gonzalo Gonzalez of San Sebastián. Stout 22"-diameter coffee basket, handled egg basket, and plain table basket for bread (right end) are by Gregorio Pabón of Ciales; dark fiber is *bejuco de cupey* and light is *bejuco de paloma* (different plants, *bejuco* meaning "vine"). Baskets are put to multiple agricultural and domestic uses, made for utility rather than for collectors. These ran $4 to $12 each in San Juan shops.

7

ON COLLECTING
TODAY

In December 1976 the Everson Museum of Art (Syracuse, New York) mounted the first major museum exhibition to cover the full range of the American folk art of basketry. Titled "Traditions in American Basketry," the 270-piece show illustrated the contributions of indigenous and immigrant cultures, as well as the work of specific groups and individuals, many of them still working but others long gone.

To call the exhibition a landmark is not at all an overstatement; the application of the word only seems pretentious if we accept the presumed "humble" nature of basketry, a proof of the dichotomy that has persisted—although it has been breaking down—between "art" and "craft" objects. Perhaps the delay in getting proper notice is not really surprising, considering the originally anonymous nature of basket-making. But the attention given to that exhibition and to lesser efforts and the appearance of several new instruction books attest to the current vitality of interest in the subject.

Fortunately, the examples chosen for inclusion in the Everson show came with documentation, which is not at all usual for objects representing a nominal investment and whose presence in a farmhouse, barn, or outbuilding would normally have been taken for granted. The collector will seldom be so fortunate as to obtain reliable provenance with his antique acquisitions. I usually have to make my own attributions.

Plates 18 and 19 show old baskets that came into my hands without satisfactory backgrounds. The sloping shoulders of the first point to Indian origin—see the Winnebago basket at the right end in figure 49—but the upholsterer's big-headed nails attaching the rim defy explanation. I do know that Plains tribes have decorated quirts and cradleboards with brass upholstery tacks. Plate 19's wide-splint basket is fascinating: it came identified as Maine Indian but looks more Scandinavian. I have seen two others of this construction but without incisions, neither with identification, and the most likely expert I contacted was as baffled as I.

There is a growing trend among today's splintworkers who cater to collectors and whose baskets are visible in exhibitions to sign or initial their pieces. Guilds of Indian Americans are encouraging identification by tagging quality examples with the artisans' names.

PRICES

With baskets making regular appearances in window displays and invading elegant advertisements for business services and Fifth Avenue fashions, even obscure little antiques shops far off from anything much are showing baskets as they wouldn't have five or ten years ago, some counting them among their specialties in listings—and at prices few could have contemplated then. Of course, as interest in any collectible spirals, prices are bound to come galloping right behind, quickly overtaking and anticipating buying pressure.

I'll not be the first to point out that it is quite understandable for private owners and dealers to want to take as favorable a view as possible of the age and quality of their holdings. Or, to put it as someone did: "People who love these things tend to be hopeful about them." It is difficult to set prices on baskets, but years of study having provided the decided advantage of having examined thousands of them, I usually know better than a seller whether a specimen's attribution makes sense and whether it's "worth" what the price tag says. So I'm ahead, if only I don't lose my head over a superb but extravagant offering, as we all must now and then.

Frances Thompson, writing on "Nashville, Tennessee, Flea Market" in the February 1977 issue of *National Antiques Review*, remarks: "Baskets have reached yet another plateau in their climb to unbelievable prices. Examples of ordinary baskets in poor condition, the same type that a year ago dealers were hesitantly pricing $5, are now tagged $18 to $22. Quality and condition seem to have little bearing on pricing." A New York City florist who handled old baskets phased them out when "the wholesale prices reached such highs that baskets became an antiques dealers' item." (It also bothered him to see good baskets ruined by people's carelessness with damp plant pots and dripping watering cans.)

I am often asked to comment upon those escalating prices and, in fact, am sometimes partially blamed for the situation. While I suppose there to be some truth in the accusation, I refuse blame where Indian baskets are concerned. All Amerind arts have become fashionable as subjects for collecting. A 1978 item in *The Indian Trader* [10] on a major auction gave prices like $1,300, $2,100, $3,500, and $4,000 for fine old Southwestern Indian baskets, many Californian, and mentioned that a large number of Apache baskets went in the $900 to $1,400 range.

It is obvious that, before moving into costly Indian baskets, it behooves a collector to do a great deal of homework. Even then he or she is wise to purchase from reliable and informed sources, particularly those who feature goods from a region about which they are thoroughly knowledgeable. I generally refuse to do tribal identifications for old baskets, on the grounds that I am not sufficiently expert. Yet I have witnessed a volunteer expert blithely assign tribal names, one after the other, to a stack of undistinguished, faded Southwestern coiled baskets offered by a hopeful collector. I thought of a lovely group of Paviotso baskets that I had come upon in Edward S. Curtis's *North American Indian* series. How many people, including that "expert," would have even heard of that tribal group, much less be able to recognize its work if they saw it?

I don't believe fine Indian baskets can fail to continue to appreciate substantially in value and I think that applies to quality new ones as well. I have in mind pieces like the Karok hat in figure 14 and some superior baskets coming out of Arizona. It is still possible to buy masterworks, for example, the imaginatively executed Hopi wickerwork plaque of the Ota kachina that is included in plate 6, but prices are elevated. Writing in the catalogue *Sacred Circles* (1977), Ralph T. Coe makes the telling comment, using as an example a beaded Plains burial outfit that represented two years of the widow's work: "Though recently completed it would cost even more than an old ethnological object, and therein lies the problem of keeping this mobile art alive; when well done, and elaborate, the work takes so long to do that it becomes completely uneconomic."

I am finding it increasingly difficult to get interesting, well-preserved, old non-Indian baskets. I've recently passed up several such with prices into the hundreds of dollars, and it is not uncommon to find quite ordinary forms with more than minimal damage going for close to one hundred. As do real estate people who stress "location, location, location," I caution "condition, condition, condition." Perfect baskets are rarely encountered, and even museums show badly worn artifacts that prove use, but I'm seeing a lot of severe damage. At a recent show, a Shaker fancy basket was offered at $95, cover and handles (holes there) missing. But as a *Business Week* personal business article on antiques put it: "When you deal with a limited quantity that grows more limited through breakage, fire, loss, and permanent collecting, each piece becomes more valuable." [11]

EDUCATION

Two of the best books on my reference shelf remain Mason and James (who dedicated his book to Mason), both listed in the Selected Bibliography, and there are other publications that proved helpful in the preparation of this volume, including some recent works. George Wharton James's Fig. 27A is a priceless photograph of the author absorbed in discoursing upon some Indian baskets to a woman and a boy. The lady is resting her head on her hand, and her expression seems to be wavering between desperation and resignation, so I suspect that the picture is of Mr. James's little family and that Mrs. James has seen and lived with quite a few baskets too many.

Basketry exhibitions, as well as how-to books and courses, are, indeed, on the rise. In 1977/78, the Field Museum of Natural History in Chicago mounted an excellent exhibition, "Basketry of the Northwest Coast Indians," and shortly afterward conducted a six-session course called "Basketry: Tradition and Technique" that had a strong staff of four and focused

> on the basketmaking traditions of three Native American culture areas —the Northwest Coast, California (Pomo), and the Southwest. The course is designed to integrate two dimensions of basketry: (1) instruction in and practice of the basic techniques of plaiting, twining and coiling; (2) the social and cultural context of the basket as art and object.

The Smithsonian Institution Traveling Exhibition Service has circulated (1977/79) the Charles W. Bowers Memorial Museum (Santa Ana, California) exhibition, "Indian Basketry of Western North America," composed of about one hundred examples from their expanding collections.

Two major 1977 exhibitions, "Sacred Circles: Two Thousand Years of North American Indian Art" at the William Rockhill Nelson Gallery and Atkins Museum of Fine Arts in Kansas City, Missouri, and "The Native American Heritage: A Survey of North American Indian Art" at The Art Institute of Chicago, incorporated much basketry. As consciousness of pride in Indianness has burgeoned, so tribal or regional cultural centers have been opening apace; these extend educational experiences for the entire family and normally feature material on handcrafts. There are countless small private museums of Indian craft arts and artifacts, often known only locally and open during limited hours or exclusively by appointment, that may offer a rare chance for personal scrutiny of individual objects.

FIGURE 82. Contemporary planter made entirely with wisteria runners by an artist-teacher, Carol Hart. An illustration of innovative application of wild or cultivated native plant material, this wickerwork basket is traditional in feeling and seems related to jardiniere forms produced early in the century in the Southern Highlands and in Liverpool, New York (fig. 61). H. 10″; L. 10½″; W. 9″.

Other than the Everson Museum's "Traditions in American Basketry" show with which we began this chapter, the only major exhibition to cover a broad range of American basketmaking was "The North American Basket 1790–1976," held at the Craft Center in Worcester, Massachusetts. Involving film programs, workshops, and lectures and supported by a grant from the National Endowment for the Arts, it consisted of both historical and contemporary baskets. In the latter category were some present-day traditional pieces, although most belonged to what author-teacher Ed Rossbach has articulated as *The New Basketry* (New York: Van Nostrand Reinhold Company, 1976). Although this craft's practitioners, usually artists skilled in many aspects of fiber work, express admiration for the products of traditional basketmakers, they prefer to strike out in other directions and achieve pieces that are more "interesting" or challenging to execute. Even when their results take container shapes, traditional basketmakers are likely to sniff at them: "Those are *baskets?*"

A contemporary planter made entirely with wisteria runners that is related in feeling to jardinieres from early in the century is shown as figure 82. Its "new-basketmaker" creator, teacher-author (*Natural Basketry*, with Dan Hart [New York: Watson-Guptill Publications, 1976]) Carol Hart, feels that the irregularities in the wisteria runners contribute to the piece's charm, whereas traditional workers strive for uniformity in their material's appearance and for symmetry of design. Although traditional artisans might turn out any number of a particular design, this basket is one of a kind.

BUILDING A COLLECTION

I'd like to suggest that it's a good idea to note immediately on a receipt any information whatsoever that comes with a basket. A separate file of these bills keeps the data safe, and then if you later decide to catalogue your collection, the information is accessible. An identifying string tag, promptly affixed to a purchase, eliminates mix-ups or memory slips. Institutions with vast collections, such as the Field Museum of Natural History, have records-retrieval systems wherein an incredible number of cross-references are set up to enter each accession. A small collector might do well to consider successively numbering each acquisition with permanent ink on the bottom of the specimen, keeping a chronological journal of acquisitions, and maintaining a card file with suitable breakdowns.

I have experienced some flushes of guilt as I fantasized frantic readers frustrated in their attempts to latch onto baskets equivalent to those I show in my books or bring to lectures. Of course, I have attended sales at which dozens of baskets were offered, but not one to tempt me, or followed leads into areas supposed to hold types I was after, only to be disappointed. But I just kept at it until I got the best to be had or determined with fair certainty that none existed. On the other hand, there can be fortuitous finds. Once, lost in New Hampshire and maddeningly dead-ended in a farmyard, my eyes lit up at the sight of baskets hanging in the barn—I had stumbled onto an antiques dealer who featured them.

Particularly when going into areas of Indian basketmaking, I dig around for whatever background and current information I can get and sit down to prepare a shopping list. (I refer to new baskets, because one is seldom substantially more likely to get antiques in the vicinity of their origin than anywhere else, the old ones having been long dispersed.) I outline research questions, too, and revise my lists as I course through the field. Some organized plan is scarcely farfetched. I recall reading that a curator for the Museum of Primitive Art in New York left for New Guinea gripping a binder containing photographs and discussions of specific types of specimens he was seeking. As these were successfully put into his boats, pages about each replaced the originals. A serious collector tries harder.

As I have long been disappointed with the quality of recent Papago baskets to be found in eastern shops, I made an opportunity to sally out onto the giant-sized Papago reservation in Arizona in late 1977. Quality and especially variety were noticeably better, but several stops were required to assemble the group in figure 25. I went into trading posts at Sells (tribal headquarters, where there is a guild), Quijotoa, and Santa Rosa. Other traders on the reservation were more remote and the area was then experiencing record downpours, so the rain-filled washes presented a stumbling block if not a danger, and I knew that some of the back roads would be impassable. Poor roads are a common impediment on back-country Indian lands.

I can vouch for the fact that it is still possible to turn up rare old baskets. *The Baskets of Rural America* pictured three museum examples of which I doubted I'd ever obtain the equivalent, but I did, and include two in this book to prove it (fig. 5 and the bonnet basket in fig. 38). Another type that I'd genuinely despaired of ever getting, having tried for years to get a good one with all the right features, I finally commissioned from an artisan.

The collector may prefer to concentrate on specific kinds of baskets. I have met a leading Santa Clara potter who sometimes barters her beautiful work for her favorite Hopi coiled (Second Mesa) baskets and has been known to collect payment for a shipment of her pots by making a sweeping selection of the best baskets on a trader's shelves.

Miniatures are gaining adherents. *House Beautiful* magazine recently reported that, among collecting hobbies, miniatures had become the third most popular in our country, surpassed only by stamps and coins. An assemblage of tiny baskets would surely save space but not searching or money, for I know a dollhouse aficionado who paid dearly for a little cheese basket. As miniatures take a disproportionate amount of time to make, it seldom really pays today's artisans to do them (but some like to). Almost a dozen tribes are represented among the miniatures illustrated in this volume, most of them new. (A bevy of miniatures makes a charming set of ornaments for a little Christmas evergreen or boxwood, or they may be mixed in with old-fashioned decorations on a big tree.)

CARE

The most important aspects of basket care, aside from the obvious one of preventing direct damage, are the elimination of wood bugs and dirt accumulation and the provision of adequate humidity to keep them from drying out, although actual dampness can be at least as destructive as chronic dryness.

Bugs in your baskets may prove a fatal ailment. One collector, upon discovery that her imported cane laundry hamper was infested with wood-eating insects, swooped it up and straightaway pitched it onto a pile of burning leaves, which was quite prudent as there was little of value lost. It is wise to inspect promptly any new acquisitions, especially those that are old or of foreign origin, remembering that coiled baskets make it easy for vermin to hide from sight. A good precaution is to toss a couple of paradichlorobenzene nuggets into suspect covered baskets and to place open baskets next to some.

Canister and tank-type vacuum cleaners with hoses often have an upholstery-brush attachment that can be handled gently to dust baskets, and a small, softer-bristled clothes brush or whisk broom is convenient for quick sweep-offs.

From spring through fall, sweet grass becomes an unofficial humidity gauge for me because, when I walk into a room where the scent is immediately noticeable, it's a sure sign that the air has a high water-vapor content. (If the intensified vanillalike scent doesn't come from a new sweet-grass decorated basket in a humid place, the material is "Hong Kong," what the Indians call an imported braided substitute.) A humidity indicator will tell whether you need to introduce extra moisture into the air. Some conservators recommend a higher year-round relative humidity than can be normally attained in a northern home in the dead of winter. And baskets should not be left where the sun can strike them directly or under a table lamp in regular use.

When storing baskets, they should be set flat on their bases, rather than being dumped haphazardly into each other; otherwise warping may occur. I buy adjustable metal standing shelf units for storage, just as museums do. You'll find that deep ones (18 inches) are more accommodating when juggling bulky baskets about, and you don't want any to extend beyond the edge, where they'll get dirt or drips from above or be bumped into. Most basements are cleaner than the upstairs, where windows, doors, people, and pets bring in an amazing amount of dirt, and placement there is a good solution because they're also out of the way. An attic is often hot and drying.

It's too easy to forget about baskets stored in the basement, so I recommend three precautions: keep paradichlorobenzene nuggets about to kill basket-chewing insects; if indicated, have a dehumidifier to control dampness outside of the heating season; and when baskets get dusty, take them outside for whisking off.

I have prowled about museum storerooms enough to know that my baskets are kept under better conditions than most of theirs. I have seen huge plastic sheets dropped over piles of baskets, and so covered with accumulated dirt that shifting them scatters grime all over oneself and everything else around; the weight could crack a brittle basket, and, in searching under there, baskets could be knocked about.

For collectors of archaeological material, reference to a paper titled "Prehistoric North American Basketry" by J. M. Adovasio [12] should prove valuable, particularly the section that takes up the cleaning and preservation of basketry remains.

DISPLAY IDEAS

For several years, I'd been watching for round, covered Indian baskets in graduated sizes to set up as a tower; the result is figure 83. And I especially like the centenarian Ohio crock stand shown on the front cover for a basket feature. With its original buttermilk paint and square-headed handmade nails, I have a much more effective display stand than an ordinary open-shelfed bookcase would be.

Among the numerous hanging, clothing, utensil, or game racks

FIGURE 83. Tower of round, covered, decorated ash-splint baskets from Eastern Woodlands tribes, stacked in graduated sizes. Covered, square or rectangular design-stamped baskets (an example appears at left in fig. 38) would be quite effective displayed in like fashion.

seen lately, any of which could have held baskets, I liked most a very old and intricate wrought-iron one of Pennsylvania German origin and a primitive-looking wooden cutout with fourteen hand-forged hooks. I've encountered others of this last sort, most with little or no ornamental incising, and the thought has occurred to me that someone a bit handy at carpentry could turn out one of original design, going to a blacksmith for the hooks. In the background of a *National Geographic* shot of a Mexican goldsmith there was a wall rack from which his small tools hung; it could be easily duplicated, consisting of a few horizontal slats with space between them, connected with verticals at the ends; his had nails for hooks, but pegs would look better. One home magazine gave directions for making a ceiling-mounted pot rack of dowels, over which S-hooks could be looped.

A New England cabinetmaker specializing in Shaker reproductions makes a finished three-foot pegboard (present in virtually every Shaker room and hallway) with pegs that were copied from those at . the Mount Lebanon Community. Smaller but similar unfinished pieces are sold in kitchen shops as mug racks, as are the expandable accordion hat-and-coat type that has more pegs, and these represent handy alternatives. Any homemade or unfinished wooden rack could be painted with old-fashioned buttermilk paint, for which I remember seeing a classified advertisement in an antiques magazine.

Just to toss off a few of the fresher display ideas noticed lately:

—A home magazine's photograph of a "waterfall" of baskets cascading down a room's corner, the largest hung near the ceiling and diminishing in size down to rivulets of small ones at the floor.

—Stepped wooden plant stands or those of circular tiers to accommodate larger baskets, library or bed steps for a small group.

—An antiques exhibiter's impromptu basket-turned-shadowbox: a rectangular splint without crossing handles turned onto its side and holding a congregation of plain Amish dolls with their richly colored toy quilts.

The owner of the lattice-sided oval basket in plate 3 has filled it with the old waxed fruit that collectors have been snapping up hungrily. (Another great find is early-nineteenth-century velvet fruit—at $180 a banana!) Yet one more thought is to show off a sturdy basket storing a gamesman's supplies, say Ping-Pong balls, in full view.

STATE OF THE ART

Anthropologists find that (quoting from the narrative text for the Field Museum's 1978 "Folk Art in China" exhibition) "In any country, the making of baskets tends to be among the last of the traditional folk arts to disappear under the impact of industrialization." The placard mentioned two pragmatic reasons: cheapness of hand manufacture and strength-to-weight ratios that are superior to those of commercial substitutes. It could have gone on to credit the traditional preference—where there is a reasonable choice—for the beauty and comforting familiarity of natural materials. But, most importantly, in much of the world craftsmen still live in poor rural villages where they can get suitable plants nearby, and, as the population shares a close interdependence because of their real or relative isolation, there is a kind of mutual captivity of supplier and consumers.

This is far from the situation in the United States today, where

114

most artisans struggle to make a living from their baskets. Civilization's substitutes are available everywhere; a plastic pan or galvanized pail costs a lot less than John Long's admirable potato basket, although Deep South oak-splint baskets are competitive (read that inexpensive), which helps to explain their persistence.

While gathering and processing wild fibers have always demanded an inordinate amount of fatiguing toil, just finding them may prove increasingly complicated for many. One artisan says his locale is experiencing a sudden building boom that may render it harder or even impossible for him to procure logs for splint.

In fact, the greatest hindrance to a more widespread practice of traditional basketry as an avocation is that of obtaining materials and preparing them. More historic villages and other museum installations would conduct basketmaking demonstrations if this were not so. Even given proximity to an oak woods, few of us are able or willing to tramp out to locate a suitable sapling, chop it down, haul back the log, section it, remove the bark, and tear it into a stock of splints with only our bare hands and a knife to start the separations. Only after, or if, we'd managed to get that far, would we be ready to sit down to try actually weaving a basket.

To begin a spruce-root basket, a Haida or Tlingit must first know where to find the right kind of trees, go and dig out the roots, cut, skin, and split them; getting the various ingredients and home-brewing her dyes is yet another job. (One basketmaker expressed the hope that this volume would include detailed information about procedures for color application, but I think that is really a separate topic better left to experienced craftworkers.) And, for all that, basketmaking is seldom a well-paid occupation. In *Spruce Root Basketry of the Alaska Tlingit* (1944), Frances Paul makes the point that, since these fine baskets were no longer made for use and never had been sold at a high enough price to pay for the time spent, a maker's satisfaction must come through pride in the skill.

Buyers find it difficult to believe the hours and tedious work involved, and even today most basketmakers are poor. One researcher found it rare for a full-time craftworker, in a tribal group for whom basketmaking was the leading craft, to earn more than a few thousand dollars a year. Two middle-aged brothers in the South Carolina Piedmont told a reporter that they figured they made about fifteen cents an hour doing oak baskets on a regular though part-time basis.[13] An excellent young Ozarks basketmaker hasn't made any for a year: "I must support myself and have never done it with baskets. So currently I am doing other types of woodwork."

Those who weave baskets now usually do so by deliberate choice. They are generally well aware that they are doing something "different," and that it may not even make good sense considering the commonly small monetary rewards or even economic sacrifice involved. I know a man who weaves wonderful splint baskets, but only in his spare time because he "couldn't live on it"; a basket that brings $32 takes him about thirty-five hours. The maker of a coiled rye-straw bee skep has estimated that one takes forty hours, even though he buys the ash binding strips already cut. He has an impressive two-year backlog of orders, including mine.

For many weavers, other than the more isolated ones, their problems do not include lack of customers, for I know any number of craftsmen who sell as fast as they produce and can't even keep samples on hand to show prospective buyers. This includes Frank Selinsky (his baskets are figs. 56, 62, pl. 11), a conscientious willow-worker who can turn them out at a fast clip but can't keep pace with demand. This book shows baskets from several living artisans who, had they been given the opportunity and chosen to join a nineteenth-century Shaker community, would surely have upheld the Shaker reputation for workmanship.

Some basketmakers are fearful that the art will be lost, commenting that young people lack the patience to learn or the industry to continue. This is a recurrent theme among Native Americans. The crux of the matter, however, rests in the availability of options for alternative employment that pays better in dollars and perhaps status. Unless they can match earnings from a factory or service job, young people will be unwilling to apprentice themselves into the craft tradition. With most of us holding baskets for enjoyment rather than their being essential in our daily activities, active economic support and personal encouragement from informed collectors will be vital in enabling more and younger workers to pursue basketmaking as their chosen career.

Most practitioners like creating a basket because it is useful and can be made or perceived as beautiful, too. But one can hardly fault the weaver who knows and values occasional recognition. I see the sweet smile and shy pride of the thirtyish Mount Pleasant crafts-woman as she replies, when a fine "fancy basket" is complimented, "I made it." Traditional American basketry, a folk art that has developed from the diversity of our origins and altered through cultural exchange, remains, in its individual aspects, singularly pure and true to the hands and eyes of the purposeful basketmaker.

NOTES

1. Don Yoder, "Folklife Studies in American Scholarship," *American Folklife*, Don Yoder, ed. (Austin, Tex., and London: University of Texas Press, 1976), essay 1.

2. Jesse D. Jennings, *Danger Cave*, Anthropological Papers, no. 27 (Salt Lake City: University of Utah Press, October 1957). Also released as Memoir 14, Society for American Archaeology, *American Antiquity*, 23, no. 2, pt. 2 (1957).

3. Florence Curtis Graybill, *Edward Sheriff Curtis: Visions of a Vanishing Race* (New York: Thomas Y. Crowell, 1976).

4. *Beautiful Tree—Chishkale,* a twenty-minute film about Southwestern Pomo (California) preparation of tanbark-oak acorns for food (American Indian Film Series, 1965).

5. Jane Green Gigli, "Dat So La Lee, Queen of the Washo Basket Makers," no. 1 in *Collected Papers on Aboriginal Basketry*, Anthropological Papers no. 16, Donald R. Tuohy and Doris L. Rendall, eds. (Carson

City, Nev.: Nevada State Museum, 1974). Originally published as Nevada State Museum Popular Series no. 3, 1967.

6. Marvin Cohodas, "Dat So La Lee's Basketry Design," *american indian art magazine* (Autumn 1976).

7. Clara Lee Tanner, *Prehistoric Southwestern Craft Arts* (Tucson, Ariz.: University of Arizona Press, 1976), p. 46.

8. Richard G. Case, "Upstate Notebook" column, *Syracuse* [N.Y.] *Herald-American*, April 4, 1976.

9. Gerald L. Davis, "Afro-American Coil Basketry in Charleston County, South Carolina: Affective Characteristics of an Artistic Craft in a Social Context," *American Folklife*, Don Yoder, ed. (Austin, Tex., and London: University of Texas Press, 1976), essay 7.

10. Kenneth R. Canfield, "Allard Auction a Success," *The Indian Trader* (May 1978), p. 27.

11. William F. Kidder, Sr., "Antiques: A Guide for Summer Collectors," a Personal Business Supplement article, *Business Week* (July 24, 1978), pp. 175–179. Reprinted by special permission; all rights reserved.

12. J. M. Adovasio, "Prehistoric North American Basketry," no. 5 in *Collected Papers on Aboriginal Basketry*, Anthropological Papers no. 16, Donald R. Tuohy and Doris L. Rendall, eds. (Carson City, Nev.: Nevada State Museum, 1974).

13. Wanda Lesley, "Shermans Put Detail into Craft," *The Greenville* [S.C.] *News and Greenville Piedmont*, September 4, 1977.

SELECTED
BIBLIOGRAPHY

BRASSER, TED J. *A Basketful of Indian Culture Change.* Canadian Ethnology Service Paper no. 22. Ottawa, Can.: National Museums of Canada, 1975.

BRIGHAM, WILLIAM T. "Mat and Basket Weaving of the Ancient (Old) Hawaiians: Described and compared with the basketry of the other Pacific Islanders." *Memoirs of the Bernice Pauahi Bishop Museum,* vol. 2, no. 1, pp. 1–105 and pls. I–XVI. Honolulu: Bishop Museum Press, 1906.

CAIN, H. THOMAS. *Pima Indian Basketry.* Phoenix, Ariz.: Heard Museum of Anthropology and Primitive Art, 1962.

COE, RALPH T. *Sacred Circles: Two Thousand Years of North American Indian Art* (catalogue of the North American showing of the exhibition). Kansas City, Mo.: William Rockhill Nelson Gallery and Atkins Museum of Fine Arts, 1977.

CURTIS, EDWARD S. *The North American Indian,* vols. 1–20 and accompanying Portfolios. Seattle, Wash., and Cambridge, Mass.: Edward S. Curtis, 1907–1930.

DAY, GREGORY. "Afro-Carolinian Art: Towards the History of a Southern Expressive Tradition." *Contemporary Art/Southeast*, 1, no. 5 (January/February 1978), pp. 17–19.

————. *South Carolina Low Country Coil Baskets* (brochure). Charleston, S.C.: Charleston Communication Center of the South Carolina Arts Commission, 1977.

ECKSTORM, FANNIE HARDY. *The Handicrafts of the Modern Indians of Maine.* Bulletin 3. Bar Harbor, Me.: Robert Abbe Museum of Stone Age Antiquities, 1932.

FALLON, CAROL. *The Art of the Indian Basket in North America* (exhibition catalogue). Miscellaneous Publication of the Museum of Art no. 99. Lawrence, Kans.: The University of Kansas Museum of Art, 1975.

GOULD, MARY EARLE. *Early American Wooden Ware & Other Kitchen Utensils.* Springfield, Mass.: The Pond-Ekberg Company, 1942 (also available as reprint from Charles E. Tuttle Company, 1962).

HOPF, CARROLL J. "Basketware of the Northeast: A Survey of the Types of Basketware Used on the Farm from the Colonial Period to 1860." Thesis submitted to the faculty of State University of New York College at Oneonta, at its Cooperstown Graduate Programs, 1965.

JAMES, GEORGE WHARTON. *Indian Basketry.* New York: Dover Publications, 1972 (an unabridged and unaltered republication of the fourth edition published in 1909 by Henry Malkan).

JONES, VOLNEY H. "Some Chippewa and Ottawa Uses of Sweet Grass." *Papers of the Michigan Academy of Scientific Arts and Letters* (for 1935), 21. Ann Arbor, Mich.: University of Michigan Press, 1936.

KISSELL, MARY LOIS. *Basketry of the Papago and Pima Indians.* Glorieta, N.M.: The Rio Grande Press, 1972 (reprint of the 1916 edition, which was issued as vol. 17, pt. 4 of *Anthropological Papers of The American Museum of Natural History*).

KROEBER, A. L. *Handbook of the Indians of California.* New York: Dover Publications, 1976 (an unabridged republication of the work originally published by the Government Printing Office, Washington, D.C., 1925, as Bulletin 78 of the Bureau of American Ethnology of the Smithsonian Institution).

LAMB, DR. FRANK W. *Indian Baskets of North America.* Riverside, Calif.: Riverside Museum Press, 1972.

LASANSKY, JEANNETTE. *Willow, Oak & Rye: Basket Traditions in Pennsylvania.* Lewisburg, Pa.: Union County Oral Traditions Projects, 1978.

MASON, OTIS TUFTON. "Aboriginal American Basketry: Studies in a Textile Art Without Machinery." *Annual Report of the Smithsonian Institution,* Report of the United States National Museum, pp. 171–548 and pls.

1–248. Washington, D.C.: 1902 (also available as reprints from The Rio Grande Press, 1971, and Peregrine Smith, 1976).

MAURER, EVAN M. *The Native American Heritage: A Survey of North American Indian Art* (catalogue of the exhibition). Chicago: The Art Institute of Chicago, 1977.

PAUL, FRANCES. *Spruce Root Basketry of the Alaska Tlingit*. Lawrence, Kans.: United States Department of the Interior, Bureau of Indian Affairs—Division of Education, 1944.

ROBINSON, BERT. *The Basket Weavers of Arizona*. Albuquerque, N.M.: University of New Mexico Press, 1954.

ROSEBERRY, VIOLA M. *Illustrated History of Indian Baskets and Plates Made by California Indians and Many Other Tribes*. Reedley, Calif.: Leo K. Brown, 1974 (a reprint of a publication showing baskets in the Lassen County Exhibit at the 1915 Panama-Pacific International Exposition in San Francisco).

ROZAIRE, CHARLES E. *Indian Basketry of Western North America* (catalogue for the circulating exhibition from the Charles W. Bowers Memorial Museum, Santa Ana, California). Los Angeles: Brooke House, 1977.

SHAPSNIKOFF, ANFESIA T., and HUDSON, RAYMOND L. "Aleut Basketry." *Anthropological Papers of the University of Alaska*, 16, no. 2, pp. 41–69. Fairbanks, Alaska: University of Alaska Press, 1974.

STEPHENSON, SUE H. *Basketry of the Appalachian Mountains*. New York: Van Nostrand Reinhold, 1977.

TANNER, CLARA LEE. *Prehistoric Southwestern Craft Arts*. Tucson, Ariz.: University of Arizona Press, 1976.

————. *Southwest Indian Craft Arts*. Tucson, Ariz.: University of Arizona Press, 1968.

TELEKI, GLORIA ROTH. *The Baskets of Rural America*. New York: E. P. Dutton & Co., Inc., 1975.

TUOHY, DONALD R., and RENDALL, DORIS L., eds. *Collected Papers on Aboriginal Basketry*. Anthropological Papers no. 16. Carson City, Nev.: Nevada State Museum in cooperation with the Nevada Archaeological Survey, 1974.

VLACH, JOHN MICHAEL. *The Afro-American Tradition in Decorative Arts* (catalogue of the exhibition). Cleveland: The Cleveland Museum of Art, 1978.

INDEX

All references are to page numbers. Those given in **boldface** *indicate illustrations and/or captions.*

125